Preface

It is a matter of great pleasure for us to present this book to our esteemed readers. This book has been designed as standard text on 'Advanced Banking & Finance (Banking Product & Services (Course Code PS572MJ)' for M.Com. (Sem. - II).

This book comprehensively covers the entire syllabus of M.Com. (Advanced Banking & Finance (Banking Product & Services) Course of Savitribai Phule Pune University effective from 2023 onwards. It has been written to meet the requirements of students of M.Com. Some of the special features of the book are as follows:

1. *Full coverage of the revised syllabus of M.Com.*
2. *Chapter outline at the beginning of each chapter to give a bird's eye view of the topics covered in the chapter.*
3. *Point wise explanation of each topic in the chapter.*
4. *Topics are logically arranged in numbered paragraphs exactly according to the modified syllabus.*
5. *Proposed questions at the end of each chapter.*
6. *Extensive use of diagrams, tables and various forms to give visual view of key concepts and techniques.*
7. *Conversational, lucid and simple language.*

Every effort has been made to provide the readers with most up-to-date and authentic material on the subject.

We are very grateful to our publisher Mrs. and Mr. Rajesh Patne who have rendered all possible assistance in bringing out this book. We wish to acknowledge our deep gratitude to staff who have assisted and helped us in preparing this book. We will consider our efforts amply rewarded in case the book proves useful to the students and teachers of the subject.

Suggestions of readers are welcome and shall be acknowledged with gratitude.

With best wishes.

By Authors

Syllabus

M.Com.- I (Sem. - II) Advanced Banking & Finance
Banking Product & Services (Course Code : PS572MJ)

Unit No.	Title with Contents	No. of Lectures
I	**Introduction**	08
	i. **Introduction** a. Traditional Banking Vs. Modern Banking. b. Investment Banking. c. Wealth Management. ii. **Insurance Products and services**: a. Life Insurance Products. b. General Insurance Products.	
II	**Digital Transformation of Indian Banking**	16
	Digital Banking - Meaning, Features and Benefits. A. Technological Developments in Banking Delivery Channels. B. Technological Developments in Payments Systems. C. **Risk & Threats in Digital Banking** i) Need & Challenges of Cyber Security. ii) National Cyber security Policy (NCSP) D. **Emerging Trends in Banking & Financial Services in India** i) Block Chain ii) Artificial Intelligence Robots iii) Digital Rupee iv) Fintech Banking v) Cloud Banking vi) Open Banking vii) Neo Bank	

INDEX

M.Com.- I (Sem. - II) Advanced Banking & Finance
Banking Product & Services (Course Code : PS572MJ)

UNIT 1 Introduction

Introduction:

The world of banking has evolved significantly over the years, transcending its traditional role of safeguarding and managing money to becoming a multifaceted industry offering a vast array of products and services designed to cater to the diverse financial needs of individuals, businesses, and institutions. In this comprehensive exploration, we will delve into the intricate landscape of banking, spanning from the foundational services of savings and checking accounts to the sophisticated realms of investment banking, digital banking, and innovative fintech solutions. Banking products and services are the lifeblood of our modern financial system, empowering us to save, invest, borrow, and transact in ways that are more convenient, secure, and efficient than ever before. This journey will take us through the core offerings of traditional banks, the disruptive forces of digital transformation, and the innovative solutions that are reshaping the future of banking, ultimately providing you with a holistic understanding of this dynamic and pivotal sector.

1.1 Traditional Banking Vs. Modern Banking:

Traditional banking relies on physical bank branches and face-to-face interactions, providing a familiar, in-person banking experience. In contrast, modern banking leverages digital channels and technology, offering 24/7 accessibility, convenience, and efficiency through online platforms and mobile apps. While traditional banking emphasizes human interaction and physical paperwork, modern banking prioritizes automation, self-service and digital security measures, ultimately catering to evolving customer preferences for convenience and accessibility in an increasingly interconnected world.

1.1.1 Traditional Banking:

Traditional banking is the conventional method of providing financial services through physical bank branches. It involves in-person customer interactions for transactions, account management, and financial advice. Paper-based processes like checks and deposit slips are common, and services are typically limited to the bank's physical locations and operating hours. Traditional banks are adapting to digital trends but retain a physical presence.

A) Meaning:

Traditional banking refers to the conventional system of financial services provided by physical banks with brick-and-mortar branches. In traditional banking, customers typically visit these physical locations to conduct various financial transactions, including opening accounts, making deposits and withdrawals, applying for loans, and seeking financial advice. This approach relies heavily on face-to-face interactions with bank staff and often involves paperwork, such as physical checks and deposit slips. Traditional banking institutions have a long history and established infrastructure, but they are increasingly adapting to modern technology to enhance their services and offer online banking options in response to evolving customer preferences.

B) Definitions:

Following are the definitions of the traditional banking:

1) Thorsten Beck:

"A system where banks primarily engage in the core functions of accepting deposits from the public and providing loans to individuals and businesses, with a focus on relationship-based lending."

2) Frederic S. Mishkin:

"The basic financial intermediation process that involves banks taking deposits from savers and channeling those funds into loans to borrowers."

3) George G. Kaufman:

"A system where banks operate as intermediaries between savers and borrowers, providing a safe place for savings and extending credit to those in need."

4) Franklin Allen and Anthony M. Santomero:

"A process in which banks transform short-term liabilities (deposits) into long-term assets (loans) while managing the associated risks."

C) Features of Traditional Banking:

Here are critical features of traditional banking:

1) Physical Branches:

One of the defining features of traditional banking is the existence of physical bank branches. These physical locations serve as hubs where customers can conduct various financial transactions, seek assistance, and access banking services. These branches are staffed with bank tellers, customer service representatives, and often financial advisors who assist customers with their banking needs.

2) **Face-to-Face Interaction:**

Traditional banking places a strong emphasis on face-to-face interactions between customers and bank staff. Customers visit bank branches to open accounts, make deposits or withdrawals, inquire about financial products, and receive personalized assistance. This interpersonal connection fosters trust and allows customers to discuss their financial goals and concerns with experienced professionals.

3) **Deposit Accounts:**

Traditional banks offer a variety of deposit accounts, including savings accounts, checking accounts, and certificates of deposit (CDs). These accounts serve as safe havens for customers to store their money securely while earning interest on their deposits. Savings and checking accounts provide easy access to funds, while CDs offer higher interest rates for longer-term savings.

4) **Lending Services:**

Traditional banks are fundamental in providing lending services to individuals and businesses. They offer a wide range of loan products, including personal loans, mortgages, auto loans, and business loans. These loans help individuals finance major purchases, such as homes and vehicles, and support businesses in expanding their operations or managing cash flow.

5) **Payment Processing:**

Traditional banks facilitate payment processing for their customers. This includes services like issuing checks, processing electronic funds transfers (EFTs), and providing wire transfer services. These mechanisms enable individuals and businesses to make payments, transfer money, and settle financial transactions efficiently.

6) **Safekeeping of Valuables:**

Some traditional banks offer safe deposit boxes for the secure storage of valuable items such as important documents, jewelry, and collectibles. These boxes provide an added layer of security and peace of mind for customers looking to protect their cherished possessions.

7) **Financial Advice:**

Traditional banks often employ financial advisors who can provide customers with guidance on a wide range of financial matters. These advisors help customers plan for retirement, invest wisely, manage debt, and make informed decisions about their financial futures. This advisory service can be particularly valuable for individuals navigating complex financial decisions.

8) Regulatory Oversight:

Traditional banks are subject to extensive regulatory oversight by government agencies, such as central banks and financial regulatory authorities. These regulations are designed to ensure the safety and soundness of the banking system, protect consumers, and maintain the stability of the broader financial market. Compliance with these regulations is a fundamental aspect of traditional banking operations.

9) Credit Assessment:

Traditional banks assess the creditworthiness of borrowers before extending credit or issuing loans. They evaluate factors such as credit history, income, and collateral to determine the risk associated with lending. This thorough credit assessment process helps mitigate the risk of loan defaults and ensures responsible lending practices.

10) Community Engagement:

Many traditional banks are deeply rooted in their local communities and actively engage in community development initiatives. They support local charities, sponsor events, and participate in community outreach programs, reinforcing their commitment to the regions they serve. This community involvement is a hallmark of traditional banking's role as a trusted financial partner.

1.1.2 Modern Banking:

Modern banking is a digital and technology-driven evolution of the traditional banking model. It leverages online platforms, mobile apps, and digital innovations to provide 24/7 accessibility, streamlined transactions, and a wide array of financial services, including online account management, mobile payments, and digital lending. Modern banking prioritizes convenience, automation, and cybersecurity, offering customers the flexibility to conduct banking activities from anywhere with internet access. It often collaborates with fintech companies to introduce innovative solutions and remains at the forefront of the evolving financial landscape.

A) Meaning:

Modern banking represents a contemporary paradigm shift in the financial industry, characterized by the widespread adoption of digital technology and innovation. It encompasses a range of online and mobile banking services, enabling customers to access, manage, and transact with their accounts anytime and anywhere. Key features of modern banking include paperless transactions, robust cybersecurity measures, and the integration of fintech solutions such as mobile payments, robo-advisors, and peer-to-peer lending. This approach emphasizes efficiency, convenience, and a seamless customer experience, fundamentally transforming the way individuals and businesses engage with their finances in the digital age.

B) Definitions:

Following are the definitions of modern banking:

1) Walter B. Wriston:

"Modern banking is banking is not a job, but a technological business."

2) John Exter:

"Modern banking is a system whereby banks create money out of nothing by the stroke of a pen, through the process of making loans."

3) John Maynard Keynes:

"Modern banking is the process by which banks create money through the extension of credit. It is a system in which the total quantity of money is not fixed, but can vary according to the actions of the banking system."

4) Charles P. Kindleberger:

"Modern banking is the nexus of relationships among banks and non-bank financial institutions, and by markets through which banks and their non-bank counterparts distribute securities."

C) Features of Modern Banking:

Modern banking has undergone significant transformations over the past few decades, driven by technological advancements, changing customer preferences, and global economic shifts. Following are the features of modern banking:

1) Digitalization and Online Banking:

Modern banking is characterized by the widespread adoption of digital technology. Online banking platforms have become the primary means for customers to access their accounts, make transactions, and manage their finances. These platforms offer features such as real-time balance updates, fund transfers, bill payments, and account statements, making banking more convenient and accessible than ever before.

2) Mobile Banking:

The rise of smartphones has led to the development of mobile banking applications. These apps enable customers to perform banking tasks on the go, providing flexibility and convenience. Features like mobile check deposits, biometric authentication (such as fingerprint or facial recognition), and notifications for account activity have revolutionized the way people interact with their banks.

3) FinTech Integration:

The integration of financial technology (FinTech) solutions into traditional banking services has been a defining feature of modern banking. Banks collaborate with FinTech startups to offer innovative products and services, including peer-to-peer lending, robo-advisors, and digital wallets. This partnership enhances efficiency, reduces costs, and expands the range of financial offerings available to customers.

4) **Data Analytics and Personalization:**

Modern banks leverage big data analytics and artificial intelligence to analyze customer data and provide personalized services. This includes tailoring product recommendations, offering customized investment portfolios, and even predicting financial needs. Data-driven insights also help banks identify potential fraud and improve risk management.

5) **Enhanced Cybersecurity:**

With the increasing reliance on digital platforms, cybersecurity has become a paramount concern for modern banking. Banks invest heavily in advanced security measures, including multi-factor authentication, encryption, and biometric verification, to protect customer data and prevent cyberattacks. Regular security audits and real-time monitoring are essential components of modern banking's cybersecurity strategy.

6) **Open Banking:**

Open banking initiatives have gained momentum in many countries, promoting the sharing of customer data between banks and authorized third-party providers. This allows customers to access a broader range of financial services and allows innovative startups to build new applications and services that integrate seamlessly with traditional banking systems.

7) **Contactless Payments and Digital Currencies:**

The advent of contactless payment methods, such as Near Field Communication (NFC) and QR code payments, has transformed how consumers make transactions. Additionally, central banks and private companies are exploring digital currencies, like cryptocurrencies and central bank digital currencies (CBDCs), which could potentially revolutionize the way money is issued and transferred.

8) **Automation and AI-Driven Customer Service:**

Automation and artificial intelligence have streamlined customer service in modern banking. Chatbots and virtual assistants provide 24/7 support, answer customer queries, and facilitate routine transactions. This not only enhances customer satisfaction but also reduces operational costs for banks.

9) **Globalization and Cross-Border Services:**

Modern banking transcends geographical boundaries. Banks offer a wide array of international services, including foreign exchange, cross-border payments, and offshore accounts. Technological advancements and global connectivity have made it easier for individuals and businesses to conduct financial transactions across borders.

10) **Sustainable Banking:**

The banking sector has increasingly recognized its role in promoting sustainability and environmental responsibility. Many modern banks incorporate Environmental,

Social, and Governance (ESG) criteria into their decision-making processes for lending and investment. Sustainable banking practices, such as green financing and impact investing, have gained prominence as banks align their strategies with societal and environmental goals.

1.1.3 Difference between Traditional Banking and Modern Banking:

Below is a comparative table illustrating the differences between traditional banking and modern banking:

Points	Traditional Banking	Modern Banking
1) Customer Interaction	Primarily in-branch interactions with limited digital access. Face-to-face communication and paper-based transactions.	Emphasizes digital platforms for transactions and services. Offers online and mobile banking for 24/7 accessibility.
2) Physical Presence	Heavily reliant on physical branches for banking services. Limited accessibility outside branch operating hours.	Reduces reliance on branches. Provides online, mobile, and ATMs for anytime, anywhere access.
3) Transaction Methods	Predominantly paper-based transactions involving checks, cash deposits, and manual paperwork.	Electronic transactions dominate, including online transfers, digital wallets, & contactless payments.
4) Service Delivery	Focuses on in-person service delivery with personalized interactions and relationship banking.	Shifts towards self-service models and AI-driven customer support. Offers tech-based solutions for efficiency and convenience.
5) Product Range	Offers traditional products like savings accounts, loans, and CDs. Limited innovation in product offerings.	Diversifies product portfolio, introducing digital banking products like robo-advisors, cryptocurrencies, & FinTech partnerships.
6) Security Measures	Relies on basic security protocols such as physical vaults and document verification.	Incorporates advanced cyber-security measures like encryption, biometrics, and AI-powered fraud detection to protect digital transactions.
7) Decision Making	Often involves manual processes and human	Implements data-driven decision-making, utilizing analytics and

	judgment in loan approvals and financial advice.	algorithms for credit scoring and personalized financial recommendations.
8) Regulatory Compliance	Complies with traditional banking regulations and faces challenges in adapting to evolving regulatory standards.	Navigates through complex regulatory frameworks while embracing innovative solutions. Strives to comply with changing regulations, such as those pertaining to digital currencies and data privacy.
9) Cost Structure	Higher operational costs due to maintaining physical branches and manual processes.	Seeks cost efficiency through digitalization, reducing overheads by promoting online services and automating routine transactions.
10) Customer Expectations	Focuses on reliability, in-person service, and long-standing relationships.	Expects convenience, speed, and personalized experiences via digital channels. Demands seamless and intuitive digital interfaces.
11) Competitive Landscape	Faces increasing competition from online banks and FinTechs but retains customer loyalty due to established brand trust.	Encounters competition from both traditional banks and innovative FinTech startups. Prioritizes innovation to stay competitive in a rapidly evolving financial landscape.

1.1.4 Similarities between Traditional Banking and Modern Banking:

Despite their differences, traditional and modern banking share some fundamental similarities:

1) **Financial Services:**

   Both traditional and modern banking institutions offer a range of financial services. They provide basic services like deposit accounts, loans, mortgages, and investment products to cater to customers' financial needs.

2) **Risk Management:**

   Both types of banks are involved in risk management practices. They assess credit risks, market risks, and operational risks to ensure the stability of their operations and safeguard customers' assets.

3) **Regulatory Compliance:**

Both traditional and modern banks operate within regulatory frameworks imposed by government authorities. They comply with regulations related to financial stability, consumer protection, anti-money laundering, and data privacy, albeit with different approaches due to their operational models.

4) **Customer Relationships:**

Both types of banks focus on establishing and maintaining customer relationships. While traditional banks may emphasize in-person relationships through branch interactions, modern banks utilize digital channels to provide personalized services and maintain customer engagement.

5) **Financial Inclusion:**

Both types of banking institutions aim to provide financial services to a wide range of customers. They strive for financial inclusion, offering banking services to individuals, businesses, and communities, albeit with varying accessibility due to the difference in operational models.

6) **Security Measures:**

Both traditional and modern banks prioritize security measures to protect customers' financial data and transactions. They employ various security protocols, encryption methods, fraud detection systems, and authentication processes to ensure the safety of financial transactions.

7) **Profit Motive:**

Both traditional and modern banks operate with the primary goal of generating profits. They aim to maximize returns on their investments, loans, and other financial services while managing risks to maintain financial stability and profitability.

8) **Intermediaries in Financial Transactions:**

Both types of banks act as intermediaries in financial transactions. They facilitate the flow of funds between savers and borrowers, providing liquidity and financial intermediation in the economy.

1.2 Investment Banking:

Investment banking is a specialized financial sector that primarily focuses on facilitating capital raising and financial advisory services for corporations, governments, and institutions. Investment banks assist clients in raising funds through activities like underwriting initial public offerings (IPOs) or issuing bonds, as well as providing mergers and acquisitions (M & A) advisory services, restructuring expertise, and strategic financial guidance. These institutions play a pivotal role in connecting investors with capital-seeking entities and often engage in trading and proprietary trading activities. Investment banking is known for its complex financial transactions, risk management, and strategic planning, making it a vital component of the global financial ecosystem.

1.2.1 Meaning:

Investment banking refers to a specialized financial sector primarily focused on providing a range of financial services to corporations, governments, and institutions. These services typically include helping clients raise capital through activities like underwriting securities or issuing bonds, offering mergers and acquisitions (M&A) advisory services, providing strategic financial guidance, and facilitating complex financial transactions. Investment banks play a critical role in connecting entities seeking capital with investors and are known for their expertise in financial markets, risk management, and complex deal structuring, making them integral players in the global financial industry.

1.2.2 Definitions:

Following are the definitions of investment banking:

1) **Benjamin Graham**:

   "Investment banking is the art of obtaining money at the lowest possible cost."

2) **Seth A. Klarman**:

   "Investment banking involves raising capital for businesses, providing advice on mergers and acquisitions, trading securities, managing investment portfolios, and executing trades."

3) **John C. Hull**:

   "Investment banking is a specialized segment of banking and financial services that focus on helping companies and governments raise capital by underwriting or acting as an intermediary in the issuance of securities."

4) **Frank J. Fabozzi**:

   "Investment banking is the financial intermediary that helps corporations, governments, and other entities raise capital by issuing debt or equity securities."

1.2.3 Features of Investment Banking:

Following are the features of investment banking:

1) **Capital Raising:**

   One of the central functions of investment banking is to facilitate capital raising for a diverse set of clients. This process involves helping companies secure financing by issuing stocks, bonds, or other securities. Investment banks act as intermediaries between the issuer (the entity raising funds) and investors, ensuring that the capital-raising process is efficient and adheres to regulatory requirements.

2) **Underwriting:**

   Investment banks often play a crucial role as underwriters in securities offerings. When a company decides to issue new shares or bonds, it faces the risk that these securities may not be fully subscribed by investors. Underwriting involves investment banks committing to purchase these securities from the issuer at a predetermined price, thus assuming the financial risk associated with the issuance. Afterward, the investment bank sells these securities to investors at market prices. This underwriting function provides issuers with a degree of certainty in their fundraising efforts.

3) **Mergers and Acquisitions (M&A):**
Investment banks are central players in the world of mergers and acquisitions (M&A). They provide advisory services to companies considering strategic transactions, such as mergers, acquisitions, divestitures, or joint ventures. Investment bankers assist in every stage of the M&A process, from initial strategic planning and target identification to due diligence, valuation, negotiation, and deal structuring. Their expertise helps clients maximize value, manage risks, and navigate the complexities of M&A transactions.

4) **Financial Advisory Services:**
Beyond M&A, investment banks offer a broad spectrum of financial advisory services. This encompasses strategic financial planning, capital allocation, corporate restructuring, and debt refinancing. Clients rely on investment banks for expert guidance in optimizing their financial strategies and enhancing their overall corporate performance. These services are tailored to the unique needs and objectives of each client.

5) **Trading and Sales:**
Many investment banks operate trading desks that engage in the buying and selling of financial instruments. These instruments include stocks, bonds, derivatives, foreign currencies, and commodities. Investment banks provide liquidity to the markets by facilitating transactions for institutional and retail clients. They employ traders and sales professionals who leverage their market expertise to execute trades on behalf of clients, manage portfolios, and offer market insights.

6) **Research and Analysis:**
Investment banks maintain dedicated research departments that produce in-depth analyses of companies, industries, and financial markets. Equity research analysts focus on dissecting the fundamentals of publicly traded companies, offering recommendations to investors on whether to buy, hold, or sell a particular stock. Fixed-income analysts assess credit risk and provide insights into bond and debt markets. These research reports are invaluable tools for investors and inform their investment decisions.

7) **Risk Management:**
Investment banks assist clients in managing various financial risks, including interest rate risk, currency risk, commodity price risk, and market volatility. They

offer a range of hedging solutions through derivatives, options, and other financial instruments. By helping clients mitigate risk, investment banks contribute to greater financial stability and security for businesses operating in uncertain economic environments.

8) **Private Equity and Venture Capital:**

Some investment banks have specialized divisions dedicated to private equity and venture capital. These divisions participate in direct investments in companies or help clients secure private equity or venture capital financing. Investment banks in this realm often take an active role in the management and governance of portfolio companies, aiming to maximize returns on investments.

9) **Global Presence:**

Leading investment banks have a global presence, maintaining offices in major financial centers worldwide. This global reach allows them to serve multinational clients effectively, provide access to diverse markets, and seize opportunities on a global scale. A global presence is essential in today's interconnected financial landscape.

10) **Regulation and Compliance:**

Investment banking operates within a heavily regulated environment. Financial regulations are designed to ensure transparency, protect investors, and maintain the stability of financial markets. Investment banks must adhere to a complex web of regulations, such as Basel III for capital adequacy, Dodd-Frank for derivatives trading, and securities laws governing securities issuance and trading. Compliance and risk management are paramount to navigate this regulatory landscape successfully.

1.2.4 Significance of Investment Banking:

Following are the significance of investment banking:

1) **Capital Rising:**

Investment banks are instrumental in raising capital for businesses and governments. They facilitate the issuance of securities such as stocks and bonds, enabling companies to access the funds they need for expansion, research and development, and other strategic initiatives. This capital infusion fuels economic growth and job creation.

2) **Mergers and Acquisitions (M&A) Advisory:**

Investment banks provide M&A advisory services to corporations seeking to buy or sell assets, merge with other companies, or restructure their operations. These transactions have a profound impact on the business landscape, allowing companies to expand their market presence, enhance efficiency, and unlock synergies. Investment banks help clients navigate the complex process of M&A, from valuation to negotiation and deal structuring.

3) **Corporate Restructuring:**

In times of financial distress, companies often require restructuring to improve their financial health. Investment banks play a crucial role in advising on debt restructurings, bankruptcy proceedings, and turnaround strategies. This expertise is essential in preserving jobs, protecting creditors' interests, and revitalizing troubled businesses.

4) **Underwriting Services:**

Investment banks act as underwriters for various types of securities offerings. They assume the risk associated with purchasing securities from issuers and reselling them to investors. This underwriting function ensures that companies can efficiently bring their securities to the market and access capital while providing a critical risk-management service.

5) **Market Making:**

Investment banks engage in market-making activities, providing liquidity to financial markets. They facilitate the buying and selling of securities, ensuring that markets remains efficient and accessible. Market makers play a vital role in narrowing bid-ask spreads, reducing price volatility, and promoting price discovery.

6) **Research and Analysis:**

Investment banks employ teams of analysts who provide in-depth research and analysis on companies, industries, and markets. Their research reports and insights are valuable to investors, helping them make informed decisions. Investment bank research also contributes to the efficient allocation of capital by providing transparency and information to the market.

7) **Risk Management:**

Investment banks offer risk management solutions to corporations and institutional clients. These solutions include derivatives, hedging strategies, and insurance products that help clients manage various risks, such as interest rate, currency, and commodity price fluctuations. Effective risk management is crucial for businesses to protect their financial stability.

8) **Global Capital Flows:**

Investment banks operate on a global scale, facilitating cross-border capital flows and international investments. They assist clients in accessing foreign markets, raising capital internationally, and navigating complex regulatory environments. This global reach fosters economic globalization and integration.

9) Innovation and Financial Engineering:

Investment banks are hubs of financial innovation and engineering. They develop complex financial products and structures that cater to the evolving needs of clients and investors. Innovations like collateralized debt obligations (CDOs), exchange-traded funds (ETFs), and structured products have transformed the financial landscape and expanded investment opportunities.

10) Economic Growth and Stability:

The activities of investment banks are closely tied to overall economic growth and stability. By facilitating capital formation, supporting M&A activity, and providing risk management tools, investment banks contribute to economic development. They also play a role in preventing financial crises by assessing and managing risk and ensuring the proper functioning of financial markets.

1.3 Wealth Management:

Wealth management is a comprehensive financial advisory service that encompasses investment management, financial planning, and personalized guidance to help individuals and families grow, preserve, and manage their wealth. Wealth managers work closely with clients to understand their financial goals, risk tolerance, and unique circumstances, crafting tailored investment portfolios and financial strategies to optimize returns while mitigating risk. These professionals offer expertise in various asset classes, tax planning, estate planning, retirement planning, and other wealth-related matters, aiming to provide holistic financial solutions that align with clients' long-term objectives, ultimately helping them achieve financial security and their desired lifestyle.

1.3.1 Meaning:

Wealth management refers to the professional financial advisory and strategic planning services aimed at assisting high-net-worth individuals, families, and organizations in effectively managing and optimizing their assets, investments, and overall financial well-being. It encompasses a broad spectrum of services, including investment portfolio management, financial planning, estate planning, tax optimization, risk management, and retirement planning. The primary goal of wealth management is to create a customized and comprehensive financial strategy that aligns with the client's specific financial goals and aspirations while ensuring prudent wealth preservation and growth over time, often provided by specialized wealth managers or advisory firms.

1.3.2 Definitions:

Following are the definitions of the wealth management:

1) Roger C. Gibson:

"Wealth Management is an integrated process for managing wealth that involves managing investments, taxes, estate planning, and risk management."

2) **Jean L.P. Brunel:**
"Wealth Management is a comprehensive and consultative process for meeting the needs and goals of affluent clients by providing the appropriate financial products and services in a coordinated way."

3) **Ralph S. Block:**
"Wealth Management is the use of a process-driven financial planning and investment advisory approach, integrating comprehensive advice, disciplined investment management, and an effective execution strategy."

4) **Michael J. Nathanson and John L. Olsen:**
"Wealth Management is a professional service that combines financial and investment advice, accounting and tax services, retirement planning, and estate planning for one fee."

5) **Mary Rowland**:
"Wealth Management is a consultative process whereby the advisor gleans from the client necessary financial information, analyzes it, and helps the client to determine what financial and investment decisions best achieve their goals."

1.3.3 Features of Wealth Management:

Wealth management is a comprehensive and intricate field that involves the management and growth of an individual's or a family's financial assets. Following are the features of wealth management:

1) **Holistic Financial Planning:**
Wealth management is centered on holistic financial planning. It involves a comprehensive assessment of an individual's or a family's financial situation, goals, and risk tolerance. This planning includes investments, taxes, estate planning, insurance, and retirement planning, ensuring a well-rounded approach to wealth preservation and growth.

2) **Client-Centric Approach:**
Wealth management is highly personalized and client-centric. Advisors work closely with clients to understand their unique financial objectives and tailor strategies accordingly. This one-on-one relationship fosters trust and enables advisors to provide tailored solutions.

3) **Diversified Investment Strategies:**
Wealth managers employ diverse investment strategies to optimize returns while managing risk. This includes allocating assets across various classes such as stocks, bonds, real estate, and alternative investments like private equity and hedge funds. Diversification helps mitigate risks associated with market volatility.

4) **Risk Management:**
Mitigating risk is a core feature of wealth management. Advisors assess a client's risk tolerance and design investment portfolios that align with their comfort level. This may involve strategies such as asset allocation, periodic rebalancing, and the use of hedging techniques.

5) **Tax Optimization:**
Wealth managers are well-versed in tax laws and regulations. They design tax-efficient investment strategies to minimize the tax burden on clients' wealth. This includes optimizing capital gains, employing tax-deferred accounts, and utilizing tax-loss harvesting.

6) **Estate Planning:**
Ensuring the smooth transfer of wealth to future generations is a crucial component of wealth management. Advisors assist clients in creating estate plans that minimize estate taxes, facilitate asset distribution, and protect family legacies. Trusts and other estate planning tools are often used for this purpose.

7) **Retirement Planning:**
Wealth management includes comprehensive retirement planning to ensure clients have a comfortable and secure retirement. Advisors help clients determine retirement goals, estimate retirement expenses, and create strategies to accumulate sufficient assets for retirement.

8) **Income Distribution:**
Managing income streams is essential, especially for retirees. Wealth managers develop strategies to optimize income distribution, which may include drawing from various investment accounts, pensions, and Social Security benefits in a tax-efficient manner.

9) **Regular Performance Monitoring:**
Wealth managers continuously monitor the performance of clients' portfolios and adjust strategies as needed. They keep clients informed about their investment progress and ensure that the financial plan remains aligned with evolving goals and market conditions.

10) **Technology Integration:**
In the digital age, technology plays a pivotal role in wealth management. Clients have access to online platforms and mobile apps to monitor their portfolios and communicate with advisors. Robo-advisors, powered by algorithms and artificial intelligence, also offer automated investment management services, often at a lower cost.

1.3.4 Significance of Wealth Management:

Following are the significance of the wealth management:

1) **Wealth Preservation:**

One of the primary goals of wealth management is to preserve the wealthy individuals and families have accumulated over time. Wealth preservation involves strategies to protect assets from risks such as market volatility, inflation, and unexpected financial setbacks. This is essential for maintaining financial security and achieving long-term financial goals.

2) **Goal Achievement:**

Wealth management helps individuals define and achieve their financial goals. Whether it's saving for retirement, funding education, buying a home, or starting a business, wealth managers create personalized financial plans that align with their clients' objectives. These plans serve as roadmaps for individuals to realize their aspirations and dreams.

3) **Investment Management:**

Wealth managers provide expert guidance on investment decisions. They design investment portfolios tailored to their clients' risk tolerance, time horizon, and financial objectives. Effective investment management aims to generate returns that outpace inflation while managing risk to avoid substantial losses.

4) **Diversification:**

Diversification is a cornerstone of wealth management. Wealth managers spread investments across different asset classes, industries, and geographic regions to reduce risk. This strategy minimizes the impact of poor-performing investments and enhances the potential for consistent returns.

5) **Tax Optimization:**

Taxes can significantly erode wealth over time. Wealth managers employ tax-efficient strategies to minimize tax liabilities, such as capital gains tax, income tax, and estate tax. These strategies may involve tax-advantaged accounts, tax-loss harvesting, and charitable giving.

6) **Risk Management:**

Wealth management includes comprehensive risk management. This entails assessing and mitigating various risks, such as market risk, credit risk, and liquidity risk. Risk management strategies aim to protect wealth from unforeseen events and financial downturns.

7) **Estate Planning:**

Estate planning is a critical aspect of wealth management. It involves the orderly transfer of assets to heirs and beneficiaries while minimizing estate taxes and administrative costs. Proper estate planning ensures that one's wealth is distributed according to their wishes and provides for the financial well-being of future generations.

8) Retirement Planning:

Wealth managers play a central role in retirement planning. They help clients determine their retirement goals, estimate retirement expenses, and create savings and investment strategies to ensure a financially secure retirement. This is particularly important as individuals are increasingly responsible for their own retirement savings.

9) Charitable Giving:

Wealth management encompasses philanthropic goals. Wealthy individuals often wish to make a positive impact through charitable giving. Wealth managers help clients structure charitable donations efficiently, maximize their charitable deductions, and create philanthropic strategies that align with their values and financial objectives.

10) Peace of Mind and Financial Confidence:

Perhaps the most intangible yet crucial aspect of wealth management is the peace of mind it offers. Knowing that one's financial affairs are in capable hands can alleviate stress and anxiety. Wealth management instills confidence in individuals, allowing them to focus on their passions and priorities rather than worrying about financial matters.

1.4 Insurance Product and Services:

Insurance products and services encompass a wide range of offerings designed to mitigate financial risks and provide protection to individuals, businesses, and assets. These offerings include life insurance, which provides financial security to beneficiaries in the event of the policyholder's death; health insurance, which covers medical expenses and healthcare-related costs; property and casualty insurance, protecting against damage to property and liability for injuries or damages; auto insurance, ensuring financial coverage in case of accidents or theft; and various specialized policies such as disability insurance, travel insurance, and pet insurance, all tailored to address specific risks and needs. Insurance services extend beyond policy issuance to include claims processing, risk assessment, policy customization, and advisory services, helping individuals and organizations make informed decisions to safeguard their financial well-being and peace of mind.

1.4.1 Life Insurance Product:

Life insurance is a financial product that provides essential protection and peace of mind to individuals and their families. By purchasing a life insurance policy, policyholders ensure that in the unfortunate event of their death, a predetermined sum of money, known as the death benefit, will be paid out to their beneficiaries. This payout can be used to replace lost income, cover funeral expenses, settle outstanding debts, and secure the financial future of loved ones. Life insurance policies come in various forms, including term life insurance, which offers coverage for a specified period, and permanent life insurance, such as whole life or universal life, which provides lifelong coverage and often includes a cash value component that can grow over time. Life insurance is a crucial tool for estate planning, income protection, and ensuring that loved ones are financially supported even when the policyholder is no longer able to provide for them.

A) Meaning:

A life insurance product is a financial arrangement between an individual and an insurance company, where the individual pays regular premiums in exchange for a contract that guarantees a predetermined sum of money, known as the death benefit, to be paid to designated beneficiaries upon the individual's death. This product serves to provide financial protection and support to the policyholder's loved ones, ensuring that they are financially secure and able to meet various financial obligations, such as replacing lost income, settling debts, covering funeral expenses, and preserving the policyholder's legacy. Life insurance products come in various forms, each offering different features and benefits to cater to individual needs and goals, making them a crucial tool in long-term financial planning and security.

B) Definitions:

Following are the definitions of the life insurance product:

1) **Jack Hungelmann**:

"Life insurance is a contract between an individual and an insurance company, where the insurance company agrees to pay a sum of money upon the death of the insured person or after a specified period of time in exchange for premium payments."

2) **David M. McCarthy**:

"Life insurance is a financial product that provides a death benefit to beneficiaries upon the death of the insured. It offers peace of mind by ensuring that loved ones are financially protected and supported, even in the absence of the primary breadwinner."

3) **Richard Taylor**:

"Life insurance is a financial instrument that transfers the risk of premature death from an individual or family to an insurance company in exchange for premium payments. It provides a financial safety net and peace of mind."

4) **Joseph M. Belth**:

"Life insurance is a contract by which one party, in consideration of a premium paid, undertakes to make periodic payments to the other, contingent on the death of the person whose life is insured."

C) Features of Life Insurance Product:

Following are the feature of life insurance product:

1) **Death Benefit**:

The primary feature of any life insurance policy is the death benefit. This is the amount of money paid to the beneficiaries (usually family members) when the policyholder passes away. It serves as a financial safety net to help cover expenses such as funeral costs, outstanding debts, and daily living expenses.

2) **Policy Types**:

Life insurance comes in various types, including term life, whole life, universal life, and variable life. Each type has distinct features and benefits. Term life insurance provides coverage for a specified term (e.g., 10, 20, or 30 years), while whole life insurance offers lifelong coverage with a cash value component.

3) **Premiums**:

Premiums are the regular payments policyholders make to maintain their life insurance coverage. Premiums can be paid annually, semi-annually, quarterly, or monthly. The amount of the premium is determined by factors such as age, health, coverage amount, and the type of policy.

4) **Cash Value**:

Whole life and some other permanent life insurance policies accumulate a cash value over time. A portion of the premium payments goes into an investment component, which grows tax-deferred. Policyholders can access this cash value through loans or withdrawals, providing a source of emergency funds or supplemental retirement income.

5) **Guaranteed and Non-Guaranteed Benefits**:

Life insurance policies often include guaranteed and non-guaranteed benefits. The death benefit is typically guaranteed, meaning it will be paid as long as premiums are paid and the policy is in force. Non-guaranteed benefits, such as dividends or interest credited to the cash value, may vary based on the insurer's financial performance.

6) **Riders**:

Riders are optional add-ons to a life insurance policy that can enhance its coverage. Common riders include accelerated death benefit riders (allowing access to a portion of the death benefit if the policyholder is diagnosed with a terminal illness), waiver of premium riders (waiving premium payments in the event of disability), and child or spousal riders (providing coverage for family members).

7) **Underwriting**:

Life insurance companies assess the risk associated with insuring an individual through a process called underwriting. Factors like age, gender, health, occupation, and lifestyle are considered when determining the premium rate. Those with lower risk profiles generally pay lower premiums.

8) **Convertible and Renewable Policies**:
Term life insurance policies often offer the option to convert to a permanent policy without undergoing a new medical exam. Renewable term policies allow policyholders to renew coverage at the end of the term without proving insurability. These features provide flexibility as insurance needs change.

9) **Estate Planning**:
Life insurance plays a crucial role in estate planning. The death benefit is typically paid tax-free to beneficiaries, helping to preserve the value of the estate and providing liquidity to cover estate taxes or other obligations. Trusts are often used in conjunction with life insurance to control the distribution of assets.

10) **Beneficiary Designation**:
Policyholders can designate one or more beneficiaries who will receive the death benefit upon their passing. Beneficiaries can be individuals, such as spouses or children, or entities like trusts or charities. It's essential to keep beneficiary designations up to date to ensure the intended recipients receive the proceeds.

D) Types of Life Insurance Product:
Life insurance products come in various forms, each designed to cater to different needs and financial goals. Here are several types of life insurance products:

1) **Term Life Insurance:**
Term life insurance offers coverage for a specified period, typically between 5 to 30 years. It provides a death benefit to beneficiaries if the insured passes away during the policy term. This type of insurance tends to be more affordable due to its temporary nature, offering straightforward coverage without cash value accumulation.

2) **Whole Life Insurance:**
Whole life insurance provides lifelong coverage and includes a savings or cash value component. It guarantees a death benefit payout and accumulates cash value over time, which policyholders can access through loans or withdrawals. Premiums are usually higher than term life insurance due to lifelong coverage and the cash value feature.

3) **Universal Life Insurance:**
Offering flexibility in premium payments and death benefits, universal life insurance builds cash value based on interest rates. Policyholders can adjust premiums and death benefits, and it provides the potential to invest in separate accounts, offering flexibility but also market-based risks.

4) **Variable Life Insurance:**
Variable life insurance allows policyholders to invest in separate accounts, providing the potential for higher returns. However, the cash value fluctuates based on

investment performance, exposing it to market risks. It offers a death benefit, but its amount can vary depending on investment performance.

5) **Indexed Universal Life Insurance:**
Indexed universal life insurance ties cash value accumulation to a market index, offering potential higher interest crediting. It combines features of universal life insurance with market-linked growth and some protection against market downturns, providing flexibility in premium and benefit adjustments.

6) **Final Expense Insurance:**
Designed to cover funeral and burial expenses, final expense insurance offers a simple application process and relatively lower coverage amounts. It serves as a means to ease the financial burden on families after the insured's passing.

7) **Guaranteed Issue Life Insurance:**
This insurance type provides coverage without medical underwriting, making it accessible to individuals with health issues or older applicants. It typically offers lower coverage amounts and may have higher premiums due to the lack of health assessments.

8) **Joint Life Insurance:**
Joint life insurance covers two individuals under a single policy, providing a death benefit upon the passing of either insured. It's commonly used in estate planning or by couples with shared financial responsibilities.

E) **Significance of Life Insurance Product:**
The importance of life insurance cannot be overstated in today's world. Life insurance products provide financial security and peace of mind to individuals and their families, helping them navigate various life stages and uncertainties. Following are the significance of life insurance product:

1) **Financial Protection:**
Life insurance serves as a crucial tool for providing financial protection to the insured's beneficiaries in the event of the policyholder's death. It ensures that loved ones can maintain their quality of life and meet financial obligations, such as mortgage payments, education expenses, and daily living expenses, even after the primary breadwinner's demise.

2) **Income Replacement:**
Life insurance plays a pivotal role in replacing the lost income of the deceased policyholder. This is especially important for families with dependents who rely on the policyholder's income to cover essential expenses. Without life insurance, the sudden loss of income can lead to financial hardship.

3) **Debt Repayment:**
Life insurance can be used to cover outstanding debts, including mortgages, car loans, and personal loans. This prevents surviving family members from being

burdened with the responsibility of repaying these debts, ensuring that they can maintain their financial stability.

4) **Estate Planning:**

Life insurance is a valuable tool for estate planning. It can help cover estate taxes and other costs associated with the transfer of assets to heirs. By providing liquidity, it ensures that assets can be distributed as intended without the need to sell valuable assets like family businesses or properties.

5) **Business Continuity:**

Life insurance is vital for business owners, as it can be used to fund buy-sell agreements and provide financial security for business partners. In the event of the death of a key person within a company, life insurance can help the business continue its operations without disruption.

6) **Legacy Planning:**

Life insurance allows individuals to leave a legacy for their loved ones or a charitable cause. It can be used to create an inheritance or make substantial donations to charitable organizations, contributing to the well-being of future generations or supporting causes that are meaningful to the policyholder.

7) **Education Funding:**

Parents often use life insurance as a means to secure their children's education. By setting up policies that mature when their children reach college age, parents can ensure that there are sufficient funds available for tuition and other educational expenses.

8) **Supplemental Retirement Income:**

Certain types of life insurance, such as whole life and universal life policies, can build cash value over time. Policyholders can access this cash value during their lifetime, providing a supplemental source of retirement income. This can be particularly valuable for individuals looking to enhance their retirement savings.

9) **Peace of Mind:**

Having life insurance can provide peace of mind to policyholders. Knowing that their loved ones will be financially protected in the event of their passing can alleviate anxiety and allow individuals to focus on their personal and professional lives without constant worry about the future.

10) **Risk Management:**

Life insurance is a crucial component of overall risk management. It helps individuals and families prepare for the unexpected and ensure that they are not caught off guard by the financial consequences of a premature death. This, in turn, promotes financial stability and resilience.

1.4.2 General Insurance Product:

General insurance, also known as non-life or property and casualty insurance, encompasses a broad spectrum of insurance products designed to provide protection against various risks and liabilities. Unlike life insurance, which focuses on providing financial security in the event of death, general insurance covers a wide range of assets and liabilities, including homes, automobiles, health, travel, businesses, and more. These policies offer coverage for unforeseen events such as accidents, natural disasters, theft, and third-party liabilities, helping individuals and businesses mitigate financial losses and maintain their financial stability in the face of unexpected events. General insurance policies typically operate on a term or annual basis, and the premiums are based on factors like the value of the insured asset, the level of coverage, and the insured's risk profile.

A) Meaning:

General insurance products refer to a wide range of insurance policies that provide coverage and protection against various non-life or property and casualty risks. These policies are designed to safeguard individuals, businesses, and assets from unexpected events such as accidents, natural disasters, theft, liability claims, and more. Unlike life insurance, which primarily focuses on financial support in the event of a person's death, general insurance is concerned with mitigating financial losses associated with damage to property, legal liabilities, or other unforeseen circumstances. These policies are typically short-term and require periodic premium payments, with the coverage and premium amount varying based on the type of insurance and individual circumstances.

B) Definitions:

Following are the definitions of the general insurance product:

1) **Kenneth S. N. Murthy:**

"General insurance is contracts that indemnify individuals, businesses, and organizations against financial losses resulting from a wide range of unforeseen events or contingencies, including accidents, natural disasters, theft, and liability claims."

2) **Dr. B. D. Gupta:**

"General insurance is financial instruments designed to mitigate financial hardships arising from risks and uncertainties other than those associated with human life. These products encompass property, casualty, liability, and health insurance."

3) **George E. Rejda:**

"General insurance is a contract that provides coverage for loss or damage to property, liability arising from various causes, and other risks that do not pertain to human life. These policies are typically short-term and offer protection against unforeseen perils."

4) Amitava Datta:

"General insurance is a category of insurance contracts that provide financial compensation or reimbursement for losses incurred due to unpredictable events, including property damage, personal injury, and third-party liabilities, except for risks associated with mortality."

C) Features of General Insurance Product:

General insurance, also known as non-life insurance, is a broad category of insurance products that offer financial protection against a range of risks and uncertainties. These policies cover a wide array of assets and liabilities, providing coverage for events that can result in financial losses.

1) Diverse Coverage:

General insurance encompasses a wide range of coverage options, including property insurance (e.g., home, business, and vehicle insurance), liability insurance (e.g., professional liability and general liability), health insurance, travel insurance, and more. This diversity allows individuals and organizations to tailor their insurance portfolios to specific needs and circumstances.

2) Risk Transfer:

One of the fundamental features of general insurance is risk transfer. Policyholders transfer the financial burden of potential losses to the insurance company in exchange for premium payments. This transfer of risk helps individuals and businesses mitigate the financial impact of unexpected events.

3) Premiums and Deductibles:

General insurance policies involve the payment of premiums by policyholders to the insurance provider. Premiums can be paid as a lump sum or in installments and are determined based on various factors, such as the type of coverage, coverage limits, deductibles, and the policyholder's risk profile. Deductibles represent the portion of a claim that the policyholder must cover before the insurance company starts reimbursing expenses.

4) Policy Terms and Conditions:

Each general insurance policy comes with its own set of terms and conditions. These terms outline the coverage details, limitations, exclusions, and obligations of both the policyholder and the insurer. Policyholders should carefully review and understand these terms to ensure they are adequately protected and comply with the policy requirements.

5) Coverage Limits:

General insurance policies specify coverage limits, which represent the maximum amount the insurer will pay out in the event of a claim. These limits vary depending on the type of coverage and the policy terms. Policyholders should assess their coverage limits to ensure they meet their financial protection needs.

6) Premium Adjustments:

Insurers may adjust premiums over time based on various factors, including changes in risk exposure, inflation, claims history, and the policyholder's circumstances. Policyholders should be aware of these potential premium adjustments and budget accordingly.

7) Claims Process:

When a covered event occurs, policyholders can file a claim to seek reimbursement for their losses. The claims process involves reporting the incident to the insurer, providing necessary documentation and evidence, and cooperating with the insurer's investigation. Timely and accurate reporting is crucial to expedite claim settlements.

8) Underwriting:

Underwriting is the process through which insurance companies evaluate the risks associated with insuring a particular individual, business, or asset. Insurers use underwriting criteria, such as age, health status, location, and past claims history, to determine premium rates and eligibility for coverage.

9) Policy Renewals:

Most general insurance policies are issued for a specified term, typically one year. At the end of each policy term, policyholders have the option to renew their coverage. Renewal premiums may be adjusted based on changes in risk factors or the policyholder's claims history. Continuous coverage is essential to maintain protection against unforeseen events.

10) Regulatory Compliance:

General insurance products are subject to regulatory oversight by government authorities to ensure fairness, transparency, and consumer protection. Insurers must comply with relevant laws and regulations, and policyholders have the right to seek recourse through regulatory bodies in case of disputes or grievances.

D) Types of General Insurance Product:

General insurance encompasses various products designed to protect against different risks. Here are several types of general insurance products:

1) Property Insurance:

Property insurance covers assets like homes and businesses. Home insurance protects against damages or losses due to fire, theft, natural disasters, and liability issues. Commercial property insurance safeguards businesses from damage or loss to physical assets such as buildings, equipment, and inventory.

2) Auto Insurance:

Comprehensive coverage within auto insurance protects vehicles from non-collision incidents like theft, vandalism, natural disasters, and accidents involving animals. Collision coverage, on the other hand, covers damages resulting from collisions with other vehicles or objects.

3) Health Insurance:

Health insurance encompasses medical coverage for illnesses, injuries, hospitalizations, surgeries, and prescription medications. Critical illness insurance offers a lump sum payment upon diagnosis of specified critical illnesses like cancer, heart attack, or stroke.

4) Liability Insurance:

Public liability insurance provides coverage against claims of third-party bodily injury or property damage occurring on the insured's premises. Professional indemnity insurance protects professionals against liabilities arising from errors, negligence, or malpractice in their services.

5) Travel Insurance:

Trip cancellation/interruption coverage reimburses non-refundable expenses if a trip is cancelled or interrupted due to covered reasons like illness, natural disasters, or flight cancellations. Medical evacuation/repatriation covers emergency medical evacuation or repatriation during travel.

6) Business Interruption Insurance:

This insurance protects businesses against financial losses resulting from a temporary shutdown due to covered perils like fire, natural disasters, or equipment breakdowns. It covers loss of income during the interruption period.

7) Marine Insurance:

Cargo insurance protects goods in transit against loss or damage during transportation. Hull insurance covers damage to vessels, boats, or ships, including machinery and equipment.

8) Cyber Insurance:

Cyber insurance protects businesses from financial losses and liabilities arising from cyberattacks, data breaches, or privacy violations. It covers costs related to ransom payments, recovery from ransomware attacks, and data breach incidents.

E) Significance of General Insurance Product:

The importance of general insurance products cannot be overstated in today's complex and uncertain world. These products play a crucial role in safeguarding individuals, businesses, and society as a whole from various risks and unexpected events.

1) Financial Protection:

One of the primary reasons for the importance of general insurance is its role in providing financial protection. General insurance products cover a wide range of risks, including damage to property, liability claims, and healthcare costs. Without this protection, individuals and businesses would be vulnerable to substantial financial losses.

2) **Risk Mitigation:**

Life is full of uncertainties, and general insurance helps individuals and organizations mitigate risks. Whether it's insuring your home, car, or business property, these policies provide a safety net that ensures that a single unfortunate event doesn't lead to financial ruin.

3) **Business Continuity:**

For businesses, general insurance is essential for ensuring continuity of operations. Insurance policies for property, liability, and business interruption help companies recover from disasters or unexpected events, reducing the potential for long-term disruption.

4) **Legal Compliance:**

In many jurisdictions, certain types of insurance coverage are mandatory. For example, auto insurance is required in most countries to legally operate a vehicle. This highlights the importance of general insurance in ensuring compliance with the law.

5) **Health and Well-being:**

Health insurance, a subset of general insurance, plays a critical role in ensuring access to healthcare services. It not only protects individuals and families from high medical expenses but also promotes overall well-being by encouraging regular check-ups and preventive care.

6) **Peace of Mind:**

Knowing that you are protected by insurance can provide peace of mind. Whether it's a homeowner sleeping soundly, knowing their home is insured against fire, or a business owner focusing on growth because they have liability coverage, insurance brings comfort and security.

7) **Risk Sharing and Pooling:**

General insurance operates on the principle of risk sharing and pooling. Many policyholders pay premiums, and a few make claims. This spreads the risk across a large group, making it more affordable for everyone. This mechanism is essential for managing catastrophic risks like natural disasters.

8) **Economic Stability:**

The insurance industry contributes significantly to economic stability. By absorbing and managing risks, insurance companies help stabilize financial markets and provide support during crises. This stabilizing effect is essential for the overall health of the economy.

9) **Innovation and Investment:**

Insurance companies often invest the premiums they collect in various assets, such as stocks and bonds. These investments generate returns that can be used to pay claims and reduce the cost of insurance for policyholders. Additionally, insurance companies drive innovation in risk assessment and management.

10) Social Welfare:

General insurance has a broader societal impact beyond individual and business protection. It helps communities and governments respond to disasters and emergencies more effectively. Insurance can facilitate the rapid recovery of affected areas and reduce the burden on public resources.

♦♦♦

Multiple Choice Questions

1) Traditional banks primarily offer ------------ services.

a) Digital b) Core c) Niche d) Advanced

2) Modern banks leverage technology for enhanced ------------.

a) Innovation b) Security c) Compliance d) Documentation

3) Traditional banks often have a physical ------------ network.

a) Digital b) Mobile c) Virtual d) Branch

4) Modern banks emphasize customer experience through user-friendly ------------ interfaces.

a) Brick-and-mortar b) Regulatory
c) Online d) In-person

5) In traditional banking, customer transactions are often carried out through ------------ methods.

a) Automated b) Mobile c) Manual d) Digital

6) Investment banks specialize in facilitating mergers and ------------.

a) Savings b) Acquisitions c) Loans d) Deposits

7) The primary function of investment banks is to raise ------------ for corporations.

a) Debt b) Equity c) Savings d) Insurance

8) Investment bankers provide advisory services for companies seeking to go ------------.

a) Public b) Private c) Digital d) Global

9) In investment banking, underwriting involves assuming the risk of ------------ securities.

a) Buying b) Selling c) Insuring d) Securing

10) The trading desks of investment banks engage in buying and selling ------------ in financial markets.

a) Stocks b) Goods c) Insurance d) Bonds

11) Wealth management focuses on personalized financial services for ----------- individuals.

a) Corporate b) High-net-worth c) Middle-class d) Young

12) Wealth managers assist clients in creating a diversified ----------- portfolio.

a) Insurance b) Banking c) Investment d) Real estate

13) Estate planning is a key component of wealth management to ensure ----------- transition.

a) Global b) Regulatory c) Smooth d) Rapid

14) Wealth managers provide advice on tax optimization and long-term ----------- strategies.

a) Spending b) Investment c) Insurance d) Saving

15) In wealth management, risk tolerance and investment goals are crucial for crafting a personalized ------------.

a) Policy b) Portfolio c) Strategy d) Contract

16) Term life insurance provides coverage for a specified ----------- period.

a) Lifetime b) Beneficiary c) Renewable d) Annual

17) Whole life insurance offers both cash value and a death ------------.

a) Benefit b) Premium c) Term d) Surrender

18) Universal life insurance allows flexibility in premium payments and accumulates ------------.

a) Deductions b) Interest c) Premiums d) Debts

19) Life insurance provides a financial ----------- to beneficiaries upon the policyholder's death.

a) Risk b) Annuity c) Benefit d) Advantage

20) Riders in life insurance policies offer additional coverage for events like ----------- or disability.

a) Retirement b) Accident c) Mortgage d) Investment

21) General insurance covers non-life assets, including property and ------------.

a) Health b) Retirement c) Wealth d) Liability

22) Auto insurance provides coverage for damage to the insured vehicle and ------------.

a) Maintenance b) Repairs c) Fuel d) Third parties

23) General insurance policies often include deductibles, which are amounts the insured must pay ------------.

a) Annually b) Initially c) Monthly d) Out-of-pocket

24) Home insurance protects against damage to the property and its ------------.

a) Business b) Portfolio c) Vehicle d) Contents

25) Liability insurance safeguards against legal claims arising from bodily injury or ------------.

a) Property damage b) Inheritance
c) Savings d) Investments

Ans : **1)** b, **2)** a, **3)** d, **4)** c, **5)** c, **6)** b, **7)** b, **8)** a, **9)** b, **10)** a, **11)** b, **12)** c, **13)** c, **14)** b, **15)** b, **16)** c, **17)** a, **18)** b, **19)** c, **20)** b, **21)** a, **22)** d, **23)** b, **24)** a, **25)** a.

Review Questions

Q.1. Answer the Following Questions.

1) What is Traditional Banking? Explain the features of Traditional Banking
2) What is mean by Modern Banking? Explain features of Modern Banking.
3) Explain the difference between Traditional Banking and Modern Banking.
4) Write the similarities between Traditional Banking and Modern Banking.
5) What is concept of Investment Banking? Explain features of Investment Banking.
6) Discuss the significance of Investment Banking.
7) What is mean by Wealth Management? Explain the features of Wealth Management.
8) Explain the importance of Wealth Management.
9) What is mean by Life Insurance? Explain the features of Life Insurance Product.
10) Explain in detail about the significance of Life Insurance Product.
11) What is of General Insurance? Explain features of General Insurance Product.
12) Explain the significance of the General Insurance Product.

Q.2. Write Short Notes on:

1) Traditional Banking.
2) Modern Banking.
3) Investment Banking.
4) Wealth Management.
5) Types of Life Insurance Product.
6) Types of General Insurance Product.

◆◆◆

UNIT 2

Digital Transformation of Indian Banking

Introduction:

The digital transformation of Indian banking has been a profound and rapid evolution, fundamentally altering the way financial services are delivered and consumed across the country. Fueled by advances in technology and changing consumer preferences, Indian banks have embraced digital channels to offer a wide array of services, including online and mobile banking, digital payments, and fintech partnerships. This transformation has expanded financial inclusion, bringing banking services to previously underserved populations, and has made transactions more convenient and efficient. Moreover, initiatives like the Unified Payments Interface (UPI) have revolutionized digital payments, making India a global leader in digital transactions. While challenges related to cybersecurity and digital literacy persists, the ongoing digital revolution in Indian banking is poised to continue reshaping the industry and driving financial accessibility and innovation for years to come.

2.1 Digital Banking:

Digital banking represents a transformative shift in the financial industry, replacing traditional brick-and-mortar banking with digital channels and technologies. It enables customers to access a comprehensive suite of financial services, including account management, payments, loans, and investments, through web and mobile applications. Digital banking not only offers unparalleled convenience and accessibility, allowing customers to conduct transactions and manage their finances anytime, anywhere, but also fosters financial inclusion by reaching previously unbanked populations. It leverages cutting-edge technologies such as artificial intelligence, blockchain, and biometrics to enhance security, streamline processes, and provide personalized experiences. As the digital banking landscape continues to evolve, it is reshaping the way individuals and businesses interact with financial institutions, making banking more efficient, customer-centric, and interconnected with the broader digital ecosystem.

2.1.1 Meaning:

Digital banking refers to the provision of traditional banking services, such as account management, transactions, loans, and payments, through digital channels and technology-driven platforms, often accessible via the internet or mobile applications. It eliminates the need for physical branch visits, enabling customers to conduct financial activities conveniently online or via their mobile devices. Digital banking leverages technological innovations to enhance efficiency, accessibility, and user experience while also enabling financial institutions to offer a broader range of services and reach a wider customer base, ultimately transforming the way people interact with their banks and manage their finances in the modern digital era.

2.1.2 Definitions:

Following are the definitions of digital banking:

1) **Bret King**:
"Digital banking is the digitization (or digital enablement) of all the traditional banking activities and programs that historically were only available to customers when physically inside of a bank branch."

2) **Chris Skinner**:
"Digital banking is the delivery of traditional banking services through digital channels such as the internet, mobile applications, and other electronic devices. It encompasses both the front-end customer experience and the back-end operational processes."

3) **Wincor Nixdorf**:
"Digital banking is a comprehensive and integrated approach to leverage digital technology to transform all the areas of banking to deliver a new and enhanced experience to customers."

4) **McKinsey & Company**:
"Digital banking refers to the end-to-end digitization of banking services, from customer interactions and transactions to the core banking processes and operations."

2.1.3 Features of Digital Banking:

Digital banking, also known as online banking or internet banking, has evolved significantly over the years, transforming the way individuals and businesses manage their finances. Following are the features of digital banking:

1) **Accessibility and Convenience:**
   Digital banking offers unparalleled accessibility and convenience. Customers can access their bank accounts and financial services 24/7 from the comfort of their homes, offices, or virtually anywhere with an internet connection. This eliminates the need for physical visits to bank branches, making banking tasks more accessible and convenient.

2) **Account Management:**
   One of the fundamental features of digital banking is the ability to manage bank accounts online. Customers can check their account balances, review transaction history, and monitor their financial activities in real-time. This transparency empowers individuals to have better control over their finances.

3) **Online Payments:**
   Digital banking facilitates various payment methods, including bill payments, fund transfers, and online shopping. Customers can pay bills, transfer money to other accounts, make loan payments, and engage in e-commerce transactions seamlessly through their digital banking platforms. Payment options often include Electronic Funds Transfer (EFT), wire transfers, and digital wallets like PayPal and Apple Pay.

4) **Mobile Banking App:**
   The advent of mobile banking applications has revolutionized digital banking. Banks and financial institutions offer user-friendly mobile apps for smartphones and tablets. These apps provide a convenient way to access banking services on the go. Customers can use mobile banking apps to check balances, transfer funds, deposit checks using mobile capture, and receive real-time alerts on their devices.

5) **Security Measures:**
   Digital banking platforms prioritize security to protect customer information and financial assets. They employ robust encryption, multi-factor authentication, and biometric verification methods (such as fingerprint or facial recognition) to ensure the safety of online transactions and account access. Regular security updates and monitoring helps detect and prevent fraudulent activities.

6) **Investment and Wealth Management:**
   Many digital banking platforms offer investment and wealth management services. Customers can access tools for trading stocks, bonds, and other securities. Additionally, robo-advisors and personalized investment portfolios are available to help individuals plan and manage their investments efficiently.

7) **Loan and Credit Services:**
   Digital banking extends to lending and credit services, allowing customers to apply for loans, mortgages, and credit cards online. The application process is streamlined, often featuring instant approvals and fund disbursements. Customers

can also monitor their loan repayment schedules and credit card transactions through the digital platform.

8) **Personal Finance Management:**

To assist customers in managing their finances effectively, digital banking platforms often include personal finance management tools. These tools may categorize expenses, set budget goals, and provide financial insights through charts and reports. Such features help customers make informed financial decisions.

9) **Customer Support and Chatbots:**

Digital banks offer customer support through various channels, including live chat, email, and phone. Additionally, many banks have integrated AI-powered chatbots that can answer frequently asked questions, guide customers through common transactions, and provide support outside regular business hours. These chatbots enhance the overall customer experience.

10) **Enhanced User Experience:**

User experience (UX) is a critical aspect of digital banking. Financial institutions invest heavily in creating intuitive and user-friendly interfaces for their online and mobile platforms. A well-designed digital banking experience includes easy navigation, responsive design, and a focus on user feedback for continuous improvement.

2.1.4 Benefits of Digital Banking:

Digital banking, also known as online banking or internet banking, has become an integral part of modern financial systems. It offers a wide range of benefits to individuals, businesses, and financial institutions alike. Following are the benefits of digital banking:

1) **Convenience and Accessibility**

One of the primary benefits of digital banking is its unparalleled convenience and accessibility. Customers can perform a wide array of banking transactions from anywhere with an internet connection, eliminating the need for physical visits to bank branches. Whether it's checking account balances, transferring funds, or paying bills, digital banking provides round-the-clock access to financial services, making it extremely convenient for individuals with busy lifestyles.

2) **Time Savings**

Digital banking saves significant amounts of time for customers. Traditional banking methods often require time-consuming trips to a bank branch, waiting in queues, and completing paperwork. With digital banking, these processes are streamlined and can be completed in a matter of minutes. Time that was once spent on banking errands can now be allocated to more productive or enjoyable activities.

3) **Cost Efficiency**

Digital banking reduces costs for both customers and financial institutions. Customers can avoid expenses associated with traveling to branches, such as fuel costs and parking fees. Additionally, many digital banking services, such as online bill payments and electronic fund transfers, are often free or offered at a lower cost than traditional alternatives. For banks, digital channels reduce the need for physical infrastructure and personnel, leading to cost savings that can be passed on to customers or reinvested in improving services.

4) **Real-Time Transaction Monitoring**

Digital banking provides customers with the ability to monitor their financial transactions in real time. This feature allows individuals to stay on top of their spending, track deposits and withdrawals, and identify any unauthorized or suspicious activities promptly. Real-time transaction monitoring enhances financial security and empowers customers to take immediate action if issues arise.

5) **Enhanced Security Measures**

Security is a paramount concern in banking, and digital banking platforms prioritize it rigorously. Banks employ advanced encryption techniques, multi-factor authentication, and biometric verification methods to safeguard customer information and financial assets. Additionally, digital platforms continuously monitor for suspicious activities and employ firewalls to protect against cyber threats. These security measures often exceed the safeguards available in traditional banking.

6) **Expanded Range of Services**

Digital banking platforms offer an extensive range of services beyond basic account management. Customers can apply for loans, mortgages, and credit cards online, often receiving instant approvals and quicker access to funds. Investment and wealth management services are also available, including stock trading, robo-advisors, and personalized investment portfolios. This expanded range of services allows customers to address various financial needs within the same digital ecosystem.

7) **Mobile Banking Apps**

Mobile banking applications have further enhanced the benefits of digital banking. Banks and financial institutions provide user-friendly mobile apps for smartphones and tablets, enabling customers to access their accounts and perform transactions on the go. These apps often feature mobile check deposit, fingerprint or facial recognition for authentication, and real-time alerts, providing a seamless and convenient banking experience.

8) **Personal Finance Management Tools**

Many digital banking platforms include personal finance management tools that empower customers to take control of their financial well-being. These tools categorize expenses, set budget goals, and provide insights into spending patterns. With a comprehensive view of their financial health, individuals can make informed decisions to improve their financial outcomes.

9) Eco-Friendly Banking

Digital banking aligns with environmentally friendly practices by reducing the need for paper-based transactions. Traditional banking often involves paperwork, including account statements, checks, and loan applications. Digital banking encourages paperless transactions, reducing the consumption of natural resources and lowering the carbon footprint associated with banking activities.

10) Accessibility to Underbanked and Unbanked Populations

Digital banking has the potential to bridge financial inclusion gaps by providing access to banking services for underbanked and unbanked populations. These individuals may not have easy access to physical bank branches but can use digital banking platforms through their smartphones or computers. This expanded access to financial services can empower marginalized communities, reduce financial disparities, and promote economic development.

2.2 Technological Development in Banking Delivery Channel:

Technological development in banking delivery channels refers to the continuous evolution and integration of digital technologies and electronic platforms within the banking sector. It encompasses the adoption of innovations such as ATMs, online and mobile banking, electronic funds transfer, and other digital tools that enhance customer accessibility, convenience, and overall banking experiences. This process aims to streamline operations, reduce costs, and broaden the range of financial services available to customers, ultimately reshaping the way banking services are delivered in the modern era by leveraging the power of technology to meet the evolving needs of consumers and businesses.

The modern service delivery formats vary significantly from the branch based model. First of all the focus is on efficiency. This means that the banks aim to provide more and more services at the least cost possible. Secondly the focus is on educating the customers and making them accustomed to banking via these new channels. Here is a list of some channels for providing banking services that have been developed recently.

1) Automated Systems:

Automated systems have become extremely popular in the past few years. This is because they generally cost less than humans performing the same service. For instance the maintenance cost of an Automated Teller Machine (ATM) is far less than that of a human teller. Also, the machine can provide service 24 by 7 which a human cannot possible do. Therefore, along with ATM's a wide variety of other automated systems have also been deployed in bank branches.

Some of the other automated system include cash deposit machine, machines which update pass books or provide bank statements or machines to recharge debit cards with predetermined values. Automates systems are now predominant in developed countries like United States and Europe where labor costs are high. These systems have also started reaching developing countries in the third world.

2) Telephone Banking:

Telephone banking is the provision of banking services over a telephone line. Therefore, telephone banking is also equipped with providing almost all the services that a traditional brick and mortar bank can. However, phone banking faces an additional challenge. Phone bankers also need to identify whether they are speaking to the correct person or else they may end up divulging sensitive information to the wrong person. Mechanisms have been created in order to ensure this. Such mechanisms include phone banking passwords and confirmation of personal information that can only be provided by the account holder.

Phone banking provides customers with extreme convenience as they can avail the service 24 by 7 and from any geographical location. Also, phone banking allows banks to reduce costs as they can outsource their call centers to lower cost countries like India where the work can be done at a fraction of the cost. Hence, a win-win situation is created.

3) Internet:

Internet banking is the provisioning of banking services over the web. Like phone banking, internet banking can be used to replicate all the services that are offered in brick and mortar branches. Also, like phone banking, identification of customers is a problem. Internet banking faces its unique sets of risks like phishing attacks and hacking of customer accounts. However, the development in technology has allowed the banks to build secure systems which can defend against such attacks.

The main reason behind the massive thrust on internet banking is that the processing capability gets transferred from bank staff to users. Hence, if a user needs a bank statement, they can obtain it themselves. The requirement of bank staff is completely eliminated and this helps the bank save massive costs. It is for this reason that banks insist on educating customers about internet banking and prefer to deal with customers in that manner. Some banks charge customers additional money if the avail a service in a brick and mortar bank branch that can also be availed online.

4) Smartphone:

Developments in information technology have made it possible for people to conduct banking transactions while on the go. The cell phones of people are connected with high speed internet. Also, mobile applications have been developed which enable customers to obtain all the services that they would be able to avail at a branch. Once again the threats of security attacks and hacking are present. However, these are risks that are being mitigated.

The banking industry believes that mobile banking of m-banking is the future of the industry wherein people will be able to avail any service they require at the click of a few buttons. Technology is therefore enabling banks to provide customers with unprecedented service levels while simultaneously providing their shareholders with unprecedented return on equity.

Technological developments in computing are certain to find more applications in the baking world. Therefore, the forerunners in the banking industry understand that their business has become intertwined with technology and the next industry leader will be someone who is able to utilize technology to the maximum.

5) **Contactless Payment Solutions:**
Contactless payment methods, utilizing NFC technology and QR codes, have gained traction. Tap-and-go payments using cards or mobile wallets and QR-based transactions offer swift and convenient payment options, especially suited for retail transactions.

6) **Artificial Intelligence (AI) Integration:**
Banks harness AI-powered chatbots and virtual assistants to provide customer support and streamline banking interactions. These systems offer personalized recommendations, answer queries, and guide customers through transactions, enhancing efficiency and customer service.

7) **Biometric Authentication Adoption:**
Biometric authentication, including fingerprint and facial recognition, has bolstered security measures in banking. These methods provide enhanced security layers, reducing reliance on traditional passwords and PINs.

8) **Open Banking Initiatives:**
Open banking frameworks facilitate secures data sharing between banks and authorized third-party financial service providers through APIs. This allows customers to access a broader range of financial products and services from multiple providers, fostering innovation and competition.

9) **Blockchain and Cryptocurrency Exploration:**
Banks explore blockchain technology and cryptocurrencies to optimize cross-border transactions, improve security, and explore potential new financial products. These innovations aim to streamline processes, reduce costs, and explore emerging market opportunities.

2.3 Technological Development in Payment Systems:

Technological development in payment systems encompasses the continuous innovation and integration of digital tools and platforms that facilitate the transfer of funds and the settlement of financial transactions. This evolution is characterized by the shift from traditional cash-based transactions to electronic and mobile payment methods, such as contactless payments, mobile wallets, and blockchain-based systems. These advancements offer greater convenience, security, and efficiency for consumers and businesses, driving a cashless society while also enabling financial inclusion for individuals who were previously underserved by traditional banking systems. As technology continues to advance, payment systems will likely become even more interconnected, interoperable, and capable of handling a wide range of financial activities, further reshaping the way we conduct financial transactions in the modern world.

1) Peer-to-Peer Payments:

Peer-to-Peer (or P2P) mode of payment involves an electronic medium through which one person transfers money to another person through an intermediary application. The funds are transferred using an online app or medium through the respective bank accounts or the credit cards of the people making the transaction. Venmo, PayPal, Apple Cash, etc. are some of the popular P2P payment apps. Advancing P2P mobile payments will improve the opportunities for businesses to monetize their products and services extensively. In fact, it is also reported that the global P2P payment market size is estimated to touch the 9.1 trillion marks by the year 2030.

2) Mobile Wallets:

Mobile wallets are similar to real wallets but in a digital form. Like you keep the wallets in your pockets or bags, these digital wallets are installed in smart devices, such as mobile phones or tablets. These digital wallets have become a fine replacement for swiping or inserting cards or keeping hard cash in your pockets. Consumers often prefer this mode of digital payment technology for its payment security and fraud prevention services. Some of the popular examples of mobile wallets are Google Pay, Apple Pay, and PayPal Wallet. The recent trends in digital wallets include the development of Bitcoin wallet solutions, the integration of QR codes for quick payments, and NFC-based technologies.

3) Electronic Payment Systems:

The continuous adoption of online shopping practices has accelerated the growth of digital payment solutions, as well. Consequently, electronic payment systems have become the most popular mode of payment, especially in the eCommerce industry. This immense popularity has forced stakeholders and business owners to re-evaluate their payment strategies and integrate online payment solutions for customers' convenience. Some common but widely used electronic payment systems include:

a) **Buy Now, Pay Later (BNPL) Solutions:**
It is a type of financing that allows customers to buy a product or service and pay later for the same over time, generally without any interest. This technique is often used by businesses to engage customers and enhance brand loyalty.

b) **eChecks:**
Electronic checks are the digital version of paper checks. eChecks use the Automated Clearing House (ACH) technique and a payment processing gateway to transfer money from a customer's checking account into the merchant's business account.

4) **Biometric Authentication:**
Biometric authentication is a method through which your payment system or device verifies a person through any of their distinguishable biological traits, such as retina scans, fingerprints, or voice recognition. In the financial domain, biometric verification is done by mobile payment apps and other digital payment solutions to authenticate transactions. For instance, when users make a transaction, the mobile payment solutions they are using share information about it along with a payment request on their devices. If enabled, the system will also ask for behavioral biometric information, successfully submission of which completes the transaction. This additional security layer makes the transaction process more robust and secure.

5) **QR Payments:**
The evolution of QR-based payment solutions opened the doors to digital transformation in the payment industry by providing a faster, simpler, and safer payment medium to customers. It's easy-to-use approach makes it one of the most popular modes of digital payments in the current landscape. In order to make a QR-based payment, all users have to do is open their bank's app or any digital wallet and scan the QR code of the merchant. They have to select any digital payment method, like a card, net banking, or Unified Payment Interface (UPI) to process and complete the transaction.

6) **Open-Banking APIs:**
Using open banking application programming interfaces, legacy banks can easily transfer data among each other with the help of third-party apps. Basically, these APIs are used by any B2B or B2C company to incorporate their products and services into a non-financial company's platform. Based on the services customers use, open banking providers can charge them and open new revenue streams. Moreover, they can also work with clients and gain insights that can be used to improve their services. However, as of 2021, only 30% of financial institutions were using open-banking APIs. The reason behind this is that most of them were already coping with the challenges related to the older tech infrastructure.

7) **Mobile Point of Sale:**
Mobile Point of Sale (or MPOS) is another popular technology that leads to digital transformation in the payments industry. It facilitates several mobile payment solutions in locations, such as parking lots, retail stores, hotels, etc. For example, a mobile POS solution allows customers to pay from any location inside a departmental store without standing in a queue at billing counters. In a similar manner, hotel staff does not need to perform formalities at the front desk to check the visitors in or out. This mobile payment trend is not only used in stores or hotels but also by SMBs or even large organizations.

8) **AI-based Voice Payments:**
After GPS navigation and mobile shopping, AI-based voice assistants are all set to help users with bill payments through an integrated voice-tracking system. AI-based voice technology will be incorporated into payment apps, transforming the future of payment technology. With this, users can leverage the AI-powered smart speakers to pay the bills using a specific set of commands, making payments convenient and seamless. It is also reported that smart speakers can be the next big thing, changing how businesses interact with their consumers.

9) **Distributed Ledger Technology:**
Several companies in the financial domain are now using distributed ledger technology (DLT) that removes the intervention of third parties from the core processes. Blockchain technology, perhaps the most popular DLT, is often used to create highly secure and tamper-proof logs of sensitive user data. This technology builds user trust, ensures transparency, and reduces transaction costs and time. Besides this, blockchain also helps businesses in reducing the processing time from several days to a few hours, especially in the case of cross-border payments.

10) **Internet of Payments (IoP):**
Being one of the services of ever-growing IoP technology, the Internet of Payments revolutionizes the banking and financial sector significantly. IoP allows fintech companies to process transactions over IoP devices, such as wearables or smart automobiles. For example, FitBit Pay, one of the features in a FitBit band, offers users to make contactless payments using tokenization. Similarly, consumers can use in-car payment apps to pay seamlessly at gas stations and parking lots – thanks to IoP transforming the automotive industry.

2.4 Risk & Threats in Digital Banking:

Digital banking faces a range of risks and threats, including cybersecurity breaches, data theft, phishing attacks and malware infections that can compromise customer information and financial assets. Moreover, the growing use of mobile banking apps exposes users to mobile-specific threats, such as mobile malware and SIM card swapping. Regulatory compliance and legal risks also loom, given the complex regulatory landscape for financial services. Additionally, as digital banking services expand, concerns regarding identity theft, social engineering, and fraud schemes continue to escalate, necessitating robust security measures, user education, and constant vigilance to safeguard the integrity and privacy of financial transactions in the digital realm.

2.4.1 Cyber Security:

Cybersecurity is the practice of safeguarding computer systems, networks, and digital assets from unauthorized access, data breaches, theft, or damage. It encompasses a wide range of technologies, processes, and best practices aimed at protecting sensitive information and maintaining the confidentiality, integrity, and availability of digital resources. In an increasingly interconnected and digitized world, cybersecurity is of paramount importance, as cyber threats such as malware, ransomware, phishing attacks, and hacking attempts continue to evolve in sophistication and frequency. Organizations and individuals must employ robust cybersecurity measures, including firewalls, encryption, multi-factor authentication, and regular security audits, to mitigate these risks and ensure the resilience of their digital infrastructure and data.

A) Meaning:

Cybersecurity refers to the practice of protecting computer systems, networks, and digital information from unauthorized access, data breaches, theft, or damage. It involves the implementation of security measures, technologies, and best practices to safeguard digital assets and ensure the confidentiality, integrity, and availability of data in an increasingly interconnected and digitized world where cyber threats such as malware, phishing attacks, and hacking attempts pose significant risks to organizations and individuals alike. The goal of cybersecurity is to establish a robust defense against these threats, thereby safeguarding the privacy, security, and functionality of digital systems and the sensitive information they contain.

B) Definitions:

Following are the definitions of cyber security:

1) NIST (National Institute of Standards and Technology):

"Cybersecurity is the practice of protecting systems, networks, and programs from digital attacks, theft, and damage, as well as ensuring the confidentiality, integrity, and availability of data."

2) Bruce Schneier:

"*Cybersecurity is about risk reduction. It involves understanding, managing, and mitigating the risks associated with digital technologies and the data they handle.*"

3) Peter Singer and Allan Friedman:

"Cybersecurity is the protection of valuable assets from unauthorized access, disruption, modification, or destruction in the cyber domain."

4) Talib Choudhry:

"Cybersecurity is the combination of processes, practices, technologies, and people that protect an organization's digital assets and ensure business continuity in the face of cyber threats."

C) Need of Cyber Security Measures:

Here are key points of need for cyber security in today's interconnected digital world:

1) Pervasive Digitalization:

In the 21st century, digital technologies have become an integral part of our daily lives and businesses. From online shopping to critical infrastructure, almost every aspect of our existence relies on digital systems. This widespread digitalization creates countless entry points for cyber threats, making cybersecurity essential to protect against potential attacks on individuals, organizations, and society at large.

2) Protecting Sensitive Data:

A significant driver for cybersecurity is the protection of sensitive and confidential data. Individuals and organizations store vast amounts of personal and financial information online, from credit card details to medical records. Cybersecurity safeguards this data from being stolen or compromised by malicious actors, preventing identity theft, fraud, and privacy violations.

3) Cybercrime on the Rise:

The prevalence of cybercrime is escalating rapidly. Hackers and cybercriminals target individuals, businesses, and governments with a wide range of attacks, including ransomware, phishing, and data breaches. The financial losses and damage to reputation caused by cybercrime underscore the urgent need for robust cybersecurity measures.

4) Protecting Critical Infrastructure:

Modern societies rely heavily on critical infrastructure such as power grids, water supplies, transportation systems, and healthcare facilities. These systems are increasingly connected to the internet, making them susceptible to cyberattacks. Effective cybersecurity is crucial to ensure the uninterrupted operation of these vital services and to prevent potential disruptions that could have catastrophic consequences.

5) Intellectual Property Protection:

Intellectual property, including patents, trade secrets, and proprietary software, represents a valuable asset for businesses and organizations. Cyberattacks aimed at stealing or compromising intellectual property can lead to significant financial losses and damage to innovation and competitiveness. Cybersecurity measures are necessary to safeguard these assets from theft or unauthorized access.

6) **Safeguarding National Security:**
Nations face cyber threats from both state-sponsored and non-state actors. Cyberattacks can target government systems, military infrastructure, and sensitive intelligence information. Effective cybersecurity is essential for protecting national security interests and preventing espionage or sabotage attempts.

7) **Privacy Preservation:**
Online privacy is a fundamental right that individuals and organizations should uphold. Cybersecurity helps protect individuals' privacy by safeguarding personal information from unauthorized access or misuse. It ensures that data is handled in compliance with privacy regulations, such as the GDPR (General Data Protection Regulation) in Europe.

8) **Protecting Financial Systems:**
The financial sector is a prime target for cybercriminals due to its wealth of valuable data and assets. Cyberattacks on banks, stock exchanges, and financial institutions can lead to financial instability and the loss of trust in the financial system. Cybersecurity measures are essential to maintain the integrity and stability of financial systems.

9) **Ensuring Business Continuity:**
Organizations rely on digital systems and networks to conduct their operations. Cyberattacks that disrupt these systems can have a profound impact on business continuity, causing financial losses and damage to reputation. Cybersecurity strategies are designed to enhance the resilience of organizations, ensuring they can continue functioning even in the face of cyber threats.

10) **Compliance with Regulations:**
Governments and regulatory bodies have recognized the importance of cyber security and have implemented various regulations and standards that organizations must comply with. Failing to meet these cybersecurity requirements can result in legal penalties, fines, and damage to an organization's reputation. Therefore, cyber security is not just a best practice but a legal obligation for many businesses.

D) **Challenges of Cyber Security:**
Here are key challenges in the field of cyber security:

1) **Evolving Cyber Threat Landscape:**
The cybersecurity landscape is in a constant state of evolution, with cybercriminals developing increasingly sophisticated and diverse attack techniques. This dynamic nature of cyber threats poses a significant challenge for organizations and security professionals who must continuously adapt and update their defenses to stay ahead of cybercriminals.

2) **Cyber Security Skills Shortage:**
There is a global shortage of skilled cybersecurity professionals. The demand for cybersecurity experts far outpaces the supply, leading to a talent gap that makes it difficult for organizations to adequately staff their security teams. This shortage increases the risk of vulnerabilities going unnoticed and creates challenges in responding to cyber incidents effectively.

3) **Rapidly Expanding Attack Surface:**
With the proliferation of internet-connected devices, the attack surface has expanded significantly. The Internet of Things (IoT), cloud computing, and mobile devices provide cybercriminals with more entry points to target. Managing and securing this vast and diverse attack surface is a formidable challenge for organizations.

4) **Insider Threats:**
Insider threats, whether intentional or unintentional, remain a significant cybersecurity challenge. Malicious employees or contractors with access to sensitive data can cause significant damage. Additionally, inadvertent actions, such as clicking on phishing links or misconfiguring security settings, can also lead to data breaches.

5) **Advanced Persistent Threats (APTs):**
APTs are highly sophisticated and stealthy cyberattacks often orchestrated by nation-states or well-funded criminal organizations. These attacks can persist for extended periods, targeting specific organizations or individuals with the goal of espionage, data theft, or sabotage. Detecting and mitigating APTs can be exceptionally challenging.

6) **Vulnerabilities in Supply Chains:**
Many organizations rely on complex supply chains and third-party vendors for various services and software components. Cybercriminals often target these supply chains, exploiting vulnerabilities to gain access to the target organization's systems. Ensuring the security of the entire supply chain is a significant challenge.

7) **Zero-Day Vulnerabilities:**
Zero-day vulnerabilities are security flaws that are unknown to the software vendor and, therefore, unpatched. Cybercriminals can exploit these vulnerabilities before patches are developed, making it difficult for organizations to defend against such attacks. Timely identification and mitigation of zero-days are critical but challenging tasks.

8) **Compliance and Regulatory Complexity:**
Organizations face a complex landscape of cybersecurity regulations and compliance requirements, such as GDPR, HIPAA, and PCI DSS. Meeting these obligations requires substantial resources and expertise, and non-compliance can result in hefty fines and legal consequences.

9) User Awareness and Training:

Human error remains one of the leading causes of security incidents. Ensuring that employees and users are educated about cybersecurity best practices and are vigilant against phishing attacks and social engineering attempts are an ongoing challenge for organizations.

10) Balancing Security and Usability:

Striking the right balance between strong security measures and user convenience is a constant challenge. Implementing overly restrictive security measures can hinder productivity and frustrate users, while overly lax security can expose organizations to risks. Finding the right equilibrium is essential but challenging.

2.4.2 National Cyber Security Policy (NCSP):

National Cyber Security Policy is a policy framework by Department of Electronics and Information Technology (DeitY) it aims at protecting the public and private infrastructure from cyber-attacks. The policy also intends to safeguard "information, such as personal information (of web users), financial and banking information and sovereign data". This was particularly relevant in the wake of US National Security Agency (NSA) leaks that suggested the US government agencies are spying on Indian users, who have no legal or technical safeguards against it. Ministry of Communications and Information Technology (India) defines Cyberspace as a complex environment consisting of interactions between people, software services supported by worldwide distribution of information and communication technology.

A) Reason for Cyber Security Policies:

India had no Cyber security policy before 2013. In 2013, *The Hindu* newspaper, citing documents leaked by NSA whistle-blower Edward Snowden, has alleged that much of the NSA surveillance was focused on India's domestic politics and its strategic and commercial interests. This sparked a furore among people. Under pressure, the government unveiled a National Cyber Security Policy 2013 on 2 July 2013.

B) Vision:

To build a secure and resilient cyberspace for citizens, business, and government and also to protect anyone from intervening in user's privacy. It mentioned a five year target of training five lakh cyber security personnel by 2018.

C) Mission:

To protect information and information infrastructure in cyberspace, build capabilities to prevent and respond to cyber threat, reduce vulnerabilities and minimize damage from cyber incidents through a combination of institutional structures, people, processes, technology, and cooperation.

D) **Objectives:**

Following are the objectives of national cyber security policy:

1) To create a secure cyber ecosystem in the country, generate adequate trust & confidence in IT systems and transactions in cyberspace and thereby enhance adoption of IT in all sectors of the economy.
2) To create an assurance framework for design of security policies and for promotion and enabling actions for compliance to global security standards and best practices by way of conformity assessment (product, process, technology & people).
3) To strengthen the Regulatory framework for ensuring a Secure Cyberspace ecosystem.
4) To enhance and create National and Sectoral level 24 x 7 mechanisms for obtaining strategic information regarding threats to ICT infrastructure, creating scenarios for response, resolution and crisis management through effective predictive, preventive, protective, response and recovery actions.
5) To enhance the protection and resilience of Nation's critical information infrastructure by operating a 24x7 National Critical Information Infrastructure Protection Centre (NCIIPC) and mandating security practices related to the design, acquisition, development, use and operation of information resources.
6) To develop suitable indigenous security technologies through frontier technology research, solution oriented research, proof of concept, pilot development, transition, diffusion and commercialisation leading to widespread deployment of secure ICT products / processes in general and specifically for addressing National Security requirements.
7) To improve visibility of the integrity of ICT products and services by establishing infrastructure for testing & validation of security of such products.
8) To create a workforce of 500,000 professionals skilled in cyber security in the next 5 years through capacity building, skill development and training.
9) To provide fiscal benefits to businesses for adoption of standard security practices and processes.
10) To enable protection of information while in process, handling, storage & transit so as to safeguard privacy of citizen's data and for reducing economic losses due to cybercrime or data theft.
11) To enable effective prevention, investigation and prosecution of cybercrime and enhancement of law enforcement capabilities through appropriate legislative intervention.
12) To create a culture of cyber security and privacy enabling responsible user behaviour & actions through an effective communication and promotion strategy.

13) To develop effective public private partnerships and collaborative engagements through technical and operational cooperation and contribution for enhancing the security of cyberspace.

14) To enhance global cooperation by promoting shared understanding and leveraging relationships for furthering the cause of security of cyberspace.

2.5 Emerging Trends in Banking & Financial Services in India:

Emerging trends in banking and financial services in India include the increasing adoption of digital banking solutions, such as mobile banking apps and digital wallets, as well as the expansion of fintech innovations like peer-to-peer lending and blockchain-based solutions. The integration of artificial intelligence and machine learning in financial operations for risk assessment, fraud detection, and customer service is also on the rise. Additionally, the Indian government's push for financial inclusion through initiatives like the Jan Dhan Yojana and the growth of online trading and investment platforms are transforming the landscape, making financial services more accessible and efficient for a wider population. Moreover, sustainable and responsible banking practices are gaining prominence as environmental and social considerations become integral to financial decision-making in India.

2.5.1 Block Chain:

Blockchain is a decentralized and immutable digital ledger technology that securely records transactions across a network of computers. It operates through a chain of blocks, each containing a batch of transactions, with new blocks added sequentially. What makes blockchain unique is its consensus mechanism, which ensures trust and transparency among participants without the need for a central authority. Transactions are cryptographically linked and time-stamped, making it extremely difficult to alter past records. This makes blockchain suitable for a wide range of applications, from cryptocurrency like Bitcoin to supply chain management, voting systems, and more, revolutionizing industries by enhancing security, traceability, and efficiency in data management and value exchange.

A) Meaning:

Blockchain is a decentralized digital ledger technology that securely records and verifies transactions across a network of computers, ensuring transparency, immutability, and trust without the need for intermediaries, making it a revolutionary tool for various industries and applications, from cryptocurrencies to supply chain management and beyond.

B) Definitions:

Following are the definitions of the block chain:

1) **Andreas M. Antonopou**:

"Blockchain is a decentralized, distributed ledger that records all transactions across a network of computers. It provides a tamper-resistant and transparent way of verifying and recording data."

2) **Melanie Swan**:

"Blockchain is a digital technology for recording and verifying transactions, enabling multiple parties to reach consensus without the need for a trusted intermediary."

3) **William Mougayar**:

"Blockchain is a global distributed database that runs on millions of devices, offering the promise of decentralization, security, transparency, and automation in various sectors beyond finance."

4) **Imran Bashir**:

"Blockchain is an adistributed, decentralized, public ledger used to record transactions across many computers." He goes on to explain its potential to disrupt various industries.

C) **Features of Block Chain:**

Following are the features of block chain:

1) **Decentralization:**

At the core of blockchain is its decentralized nature. Unlike traditional centralized systems where a single entity or authority controls the data, blockchain operates on a network of computers (nodes) distributed worldwide. This decentralization ensures that no single entity has ultimate control, making it resistant to censorship and single points of failure.

2) **Transparency:**

Blockchain is often described as a transparent and open ledger. All transactions that occur on the blockchain are visible to all participants in the network. This transparency fosters trust among users, as they can independently verify and audit transactions.

3) **Immutability:**

Once data is recorded on a blockchain, it becomes extremely difficult to alter or delete. Each block contains a cryptographic reference to the previous block, creating a chain of blocks (hence the name). This immutability ensures the integrity of historical data, making blockchain a secure and tamper-resistant technology.

4) **Security through Cryptography:**

Blockchain uses advanced cryptographic techniques to secure data. Each transaction is digitally signed, and consensus mechanisms ensure that only valid transactions are added to the ledger. This cryptographic layer provides robust protection against fraud and unauthorized access.

5) Consensus Mechanisms:

Blockchains rely on consensus mechanisms to validate and add new transactions to the ledger. The most well-known mechanism is Proof of Work (PoW), used in Bitcoin, and Proof of Stake (PoS), employed in various other blockchains. These mechanisms ensure that the majority of network participants agree on the state of the ledger, enhancing security and preventing double-spending.

6) Smart Contracts:

Some blockchains, such as Ethereum, support smart contracts, which are self-executing contracts with predefined rules and conditions. Smart contracts automate processes, enabling trustless and tamper-proof execution of agreements. They find applications in areas like finance, supply chain management, and legal contracts.

7) Trustless Transactions:

Blockchain enables trustless transactions, meaning that parties can engage in transactions without the need for trust in a central authority or intermediary. The blockchain's consensus mechanisms and cryptographic security make trustless interactions possible.

8) Pseudonymity:

While blockchain transactions are transparent, they are also pseudonymous. Instead of real-world identities, users are represented by cryptographic addresses. This provides a degree of privacy while maintaining transparency.

9) Reduced Intermediaries:

Blockchain eliminates the need for many intermediaries in various processes, such as financial transactions, supply chain management, and legal agreements. This reduction in intermediaries can result in cost savings, faster processes, and fewer opportunities for errors or fraud.

10) Potential for Tokenization:

Blockchain facilitates the creation of digital tokens that can represent a wide range of assets, including cryptocurrencies, real estate, art, and more. These tokens can be easily traded, divided, and transferred, increasing liquidity and accessibility to assets.

D) Challenges of Block Chain:

Here are the challenges and limitations of block chain:

1) Scalability:

Blockchain networks, especially those using Proof of Work (PoW) consensus mechanisms like Bitcoin and Ethereum, often struggle with scalability. The limited number of transactions that can be processed per second (TPS) and the time it takes to confirm transactions hinder their ability to handle the volume and speed required for widespread adoption. As more users and applications join the network, scalability issues become more pronounced.

2) **Energy Consumption:**

PoW blockchains, which are prevalent in the industry, consume a significant amount of energy. Mining, the process of validating and adding transactions to the blockchain, requires extensive computational power. This high energy consumption has raised environmental concerns, particularly regarding carbon emissions and sustainability.

3) **Regulatory Uncertainty:**

Blockchain technology operates in a legal and regulatory landscape that varies widely from one jurisdiction to another. The lack of consistent, clear, and globally recognized regulations creates uncertainty for businesses and users alike. Issues such as taxation, data protection, and securities regulation are particularly challenging to navigate.

4) **Interoperability:**

The blockchain ecosystem is fragmented, with numerous blockchains and protocols in existence, each with its own set of rules and standards. Achieving interoperability between these diverse networks is challenging. It's crucial for blockchain technology to facilitate seamless data and asset transfer between different blockchains for it to fulfill its potential.

5) **Privacy Concerns:**

While blockchain transactions are pseudonymous, they are also transparent and permanently recorded on the ledger. This transparency can be a challenge for applications that require confidentiality or privacy, such as healthcare and sensitive financial transactions. Balancing transparency and privacy is a complex issue.

6) **User-Friendliness:**

Many blockchain and cryptocurrency interfaces remain complex and difficult for non-technical users to navigate. This complexity hinders mass adoption and requires efforts to improve user-friendliness in terms of wallets, key management, and overall user experience.

7) **Legal Challenges:**

Smart contracts, which automate and execute agreements on the blockchain, raise legal challenges. The enforceability of smart contracts in traditional legal systems, the resolution of disputes, and the legal status of blockchain-based assets are areas of concern.

8) **Security Vulnerabilities:**

While blockchain is renowned for its security, it's not immune to vulnerabilities. Smart contract bugs, 51% attacks, and vulnerabilities in wallet software have led to significant losses in the past. Continuous efforts are required to enhance security and protect users.

9) Adoption Hurdles:

Widespread adoption of blockchain technology faces resistance from legacy systems, established institutions, and businesses invested in traditional processes. Transitioning to blockchain requires significant changes and investments in infrastructure, training, and cultural shifts.

10) Lack of Understanding:

A lack of understanding and knowledge about blockchain technology among the general population and decision-makers is a significant challenge. Misconceptions, hype, and the complexity of the technology hinder informed decision-making and investment.

2.5.2 Artificial Intelligence Robots:

Artificial intelligence robots represent the pinnacle of technological innovation, combining sophisticated algorithms and machine learning capabilities with physical bodies to interact with and navigate the real world. These robots possess the ability to perceive their environment through sensors, process vast amounts of data to make intelligent decisions, and execute tasks autonomously. From humanoid robots that assist in healthcare and customer service to autonomous vehicles revolutionizing transportation, AI robots are at the forefront of reshaping industries and daily life, promising efficiency, precision, and new possibilities while also sparking discussions about ethical and societal implications in the era of automation and intelligent machines.

A) Meaning:

Artificial intelligence robots, often referred to as AI robots, are advanced machines equipped with AI technologies that enable them to perceive their environment, make intelligent decisions, and execute tasks with varying degrees of autonomy. These robots are designed to mimic human cognitive functions, such as learning, problem-solving, and decision-making, and can be employed in a wide range of applications, from manufacturing and healthcare to autonomous vehicles and customer service. They represent a convergence of robotics and AI, promising to enhance efficiency, productivity, and innovation across industries, while also raising important ethical and societal questions about their impact on employment, privacy, and human-machine interactions.

B) Definitions:

Following are the definitions of the artificial intelligence:

1) **Stuart Russell**:

"AI robots are the study of how to make computers do things at which, at the moment, people are better."

2) **Rodney Brooks**:

"AI robots are machines that can perceive their environment, reason about it, and take actions to achieve specific goals."

3) **Elon Musk:**

"AI robots are computers that can outperform human's at most economically valuable work."

4) **Andrew Ng:**

"AI robots are machines that are capable of learning from data and making decisions or taking actions based on that learning."

C) **Features of Artificial Intelligence Robots:**

Following are the features of artificial intelligence robots:

1) **Sensing and Perception:**

AI robots are equipped with a wide range of sensors, including cameras, microphones, lidar, radar, and touch sensors, allowing them to perceive and interpret their surroundings. These sensors enable robots to gather data about their environment, detect objects, and sense changes in their surroundings.

2) **Machine Learning and Adaptability:**

AI robots leverage machine learning algorithms to acquire knowledge and adapt to changing conditions. They can learn from data and experiences, improving their performance over time. This adaptability allows them to handle new tasks and environments effectively.

3) **Autonomy and Decision-Making:**

AI robots possess varying levels of autonomy, from semi-autonomous to fully autonomous. They can make decisions based on their sensor data and learned models, enabling them to navigate complex environments, avoid obstacles, and perform tasks without constant human intervention.

4) **Natural Language Processing (NLP):**

Many AI robots are equipped with NLP capabilities, enabling them to understand and respond to human language. This feature enables natural and intuitive interactions with users, making them suitable for customer service, companionship, and information retrieval.

5) **Computer Vision:**

Computer vision is a fundamental feature of AI robots, allowing them to interpret visual information from cameras and other sensors. This capability enables robots to recognize objects, people, gestures, and facial expressions, facilitating tasks like facial recognition, object manipulation, and navigation.

6) **Object Manipulation and Dexterity:**

Advanced AI robots possess dexterous manipulators, such as robotic arms with multiple degrees of freedom and precision grippers. These robots can manipulate objects with precision, performing tasks like assembly, picking and placing, and even delicate surgical procedures.

7) Learning from Demonstrations (LfD):

LfD is a feature that enables AI robots to learn tasks by observing and imitating human demonstrations. This capability streamlines the training process and makes robots more accessible for users without specialized programming skills.

8) Multi-Modal Perception:

AI robots integrate data from multiple sensory modalities, such as vision, audio, and touch, to form a holistic understanding of their environment. This multi-modal perception enhances their ability to interact with the world and adapt to complex scenarios.

9) Human-Robot Collaboration:

AI robots are designed for collaboration with humans in various contexts, including manufacturing, healthcare, and research. They can work alongside humans, assisting with tasks, enhancing productivity, and ensuring safety through sensors and decision-making capabilities.

10) Ethical Considerations and Safety:

AI robots are programmed to adhere to ethical guidelines and safety protocols. These include avoiding harm to humans, respecting privacy, and following legal and ethical principles. Ensuring the ethical and responsible use of AI robots is a crucial feature in their development and deployment.

D) Challenges of Artificial Intelligence Robots:

Following are the challenges of artificial intelligence robots:

1) Ethical and Moral Dilemmas:

As AI robots become more autonomous and capable of making decisions, ethical dilemmas arise. Questions about robot rights, accountability for robot actions, and the potential for robots to make morally ambiguous decisions are complex and require careful consideration.

2) Job Displacement and Employment:

The automation of tasks by AI robots has the potential to disrupt labor markets and lead to job displacement in certain industries. Preparing the workforce for these changes and addressing the economic implications are significant challenges.

3) Safety and Security:

Ensuring the safety of AI robots and preventing malicious use or hacking of robots are major concerns. Malware or cyberattacks on robots could lead to physical harm, data breaches, or unauthorized access to sensitive information.

4) Privacy:

AI robots equipped with cameras and sensors can raise privacy concerns when used in public or private spaces. Balancing the benefits of data collection for robot functionality with individual privacy rights is an ongoing challenge.

5) **Bias and Fairness:**

AI robots can inherit biases from the data they are trained on, leading to biased decision-making or discriminatory outcomes. Addressing bias and ensuring fairness in AI algorithms is crucial to prevent unfair treatment and reinforce societal biases.

6) **Limited Understanding of AI Decision-Making:**

The complexity of AI algorithms, particularly in deep learning models, can make it difficult to understand how robots arrive at specific decisions or actions. Explainability and transparency in AI decision-making are areas that require further development.

7) **Regulation and Standardization:**

The lack of consistent regulations and standards for AI robots creates uncertainty and challenges in areas such as safety, liability, and interoperability. Developing a regulatory framework that balances innovation and safety is essential.

8) **Human-Robot Interaction:**

Designing intuitive and effective human-robot interfaces and ensuring smooth human-robot collaboration are ongoing challenges. Robots must be able to understand and respond to human cues and instructions effectively.

9) **Cost and Accessibility:**

Developing and deploying AI robots can be expensive, limiting access to this technology for certain individuals or organizations. Reducing costs and increasing accessibility are important goals for wider adoption.

10) **Long-Term Autonomy:**

Achieving long-term autonomy in AI robots, where they can operate reliably for extended periods without human intervention, remains a challenge. Maintenance, power sources, and robustness in complex environments are key factors to address.

2.5.3 Digital Rupee:

A digital rupee refers to a digital representation of the Indian national currency, the Indian Rupee (INR), which exists purely in digital form and is issued and regulated by the Reserve Bank of India (RBI). This digital currency, often referred to as a Central Bank Digital Currency (CBDC), is designed to enable secure and efficient electronic transactions, offering a cashless alternative to physical currency. It is poised to revolutionize the Indian financial landscape by enhancing financial inclusion, reducing the cost of cash management, and potentially enabling new financial services and innovations while also raising questions about privacy, cybersecurity, and regulatory implications in the digital economy.

A) Meaning:

The term "digital rupee" refers to a digital representation of the Indian Rupee (INR), the official currency of India, which is issued and regulated by the Reserve Bank of India (RBI). This digital form of the currency exists solely in electronic or digital format, allowing for secure, instant, and trackable transactions in the digital realm. It is a form of Central Bank Digital Currency (CBDC) designed to facilitate digital payments and financial transactions, potentially reducing the reliance on physical cash and offering a more efficient means of conducting electronic commerce within the country.

B) Features of Digital Rupee:

A digital rupee is a transformative concept in the realm of digital finance and central banking. Following are the features of digital rupee:

1) Central Bank Backing:

A digital rupee would be issued and regulated by the Reserve Bank of India (RBI), providing it with the same level of trust and stability as physical rupees. This central bank backing ensures that it retains its value and reliability in the digital realm.

2) Digital Infrastructure:

To facilitate the use of a digital rupee, a robust digital infrastructure would be required. This would include secure servers, encryption protocols, and authentication mechanisms to ensure the security and integrity of digital transactions.

3) Blockchain or DLT Technology:

Many discussions about digital currencies involve blockchain or distributed ledger technology (DLT) as the underlying infrastructure. This technology can provide transparency, immutability, and security to transactions, making it suitable for a digital rupee. However, other technologies might also be considered.

4) Accessibility and Inclusivity:

One of the primary goals of introducing a digital rupee is to increase financial inclusion. It should be easily accessible to all citizens, including those in remote areas or with limited access to traditional banking services. Mobile apps, internet access, and user-friendly interfaces would play a crucial role in achieving this goal.

5) Privacy and Security:

A digital rupee system must prioritize user privacy and security. Transaction data should be protected against unauthorized access, and users should have control over their personal information. At the same time, it should incorporate security measures to prevent fraud and cyberattacks.

6) Interoperability:

A digital rupee system should be interoperable with existing payment systems and financial institutions. It should seamlessly integrate with other digital payment platforms, allowing users to transfer funds between traditional bank accounts and digital wallets.

7) **Cross-Border Transactions:**

Facilitating cross-border transactions is a significant advantage of digital currencies. A digital rupee should have mechanisms in place to enable international transactions and trade, reducing the reliance on traditional remittance services and foreign exchange intermediaries.

8) **Smart Contracts and Programmability:**

If built on a blockchain or similar technology, a digital rupee could support smart contracts. These self-executing contracts can automate various financial processes, from payments to agreements, creating efficiency and reducing the need for intermediaries.

9) **Monetary Policy Implementation:**

The introduction of a digital rupee would require careful consideration of its impact on monetary policy. The RBI would need mechanisms to control the supply and circulation of digital rupees to maintain price stability and control inflation.

10) **Financial Innovation and Economic Impact:**

A digital rupee has the potential to drive financial innovation and transform the Indian economy. It can foster the development of new fintech services and payment solutions, leading to greater economic efficiency and growth.

C) **Challenges of Digital Rupee:**

The introduction of a digital rupee, like any major financial innovation, would come with various challenges and considerations. Following are the challenges of digital rupee:

1) **Security and Cybersecurity Risks:**

Implementing a digital rupee would expose the financial system to new cybersecurity threats. Hackers and cybercriminals may attempt to breach the digital infrastructure, steal user data, or manipulate transactions. Ensuring the highest level of security would be imperative to protect the digital currency and its users.

2) **User Privacy Concerns:**

Balancing user privacy with regulatory requirements is a challenge. While ensuring transparency and compliance with anti-money laundering (AML) and know-your-customer (KYC) regulations is essential, users' privacy rights must be respected. Striking this balance is a complex task.

3) **Financial Inclusion and Accessibility:**

While the digital rupee aims to promote financial inclusion, ensuring that it is accessible to all segments of society can be challenging. Many parts of India still lack reliable internet access and digital literacy, which could exclude certain populations from using the digital currency.

4) **Interoperability with Existing Systems:**
Integrating the digital rupee with existing payment systems and financial institutions may be complex. Ensuring interoperability to facilitate seamless transactions between digital wallets, traditional bank accounts, and other payment platforms requires careful planning and coordination.

5) **Fraud Prevention and Consumer Protection:**
With the transition to digital payments, there is a risk of increased fraud and scams. Educating users on safe practices and implementing strong fraud prevention measures would be crucial to protect consumers.

6) **Monetary Policy and Inflation Control:**
The RBI would need to adapt its monetary policy tools to manage the supply and circulation of the digital rupee effectively. Failure to do so could impact inflation control and financial stability.

7) **Digital Infrastructure and Connectivity:** Many areas in India still lack reliable internet connectivity and digital infrastructure. Ensuring that even remote regions have access to the digital rupee is essential for financial inclusion. Infrastructure investments and expansion efforts would be necessary.

8) **Cross-Border Transactions and Regulatory Coordination:**
Facilitating cross-border transactions with a digital rupee could be complicated due to varying international regulations. Ensuring that it complies with global standards and establishing international regulatory coordination are essential for seamless cross-border transactions.

9) **Education and Awareness:**
To encourage the adoption of the digital rupee, a significant effort would be needed to educate the public about its benefits, usage, and security practices. Users must have a clear understanding of how to use the digital currency safely and effectively.

10) **Resistance to Change:**
Transitioning to a digital rupee may face resistance from various stakeholders, including traditional financial institutions and individuals who are accustomed to using physical cash. Addressing these concerns and fostering trust in the digital currency would be vital for its success.

2.5.4 Fintech Banking:

Fintech banking, short for financial technology banking refers to the innovative use of technology in financial services. It encompasses online banking, digital payments, peer-to-peer lending, and robo-advisors, among other services. Fintech banks often operate without physical branches, offering customers convenient, tech-driven solutions for managing their finances. This sector has disrupted traditional banking, enhancing accessibility, speed and efficiency in financial transactions and services.

A) Meaning:

Fintech banking, or financial technology banking, is a modern approach to providing financial services that leverages innovative technology to offer efficient, accessible, and customer-centric solutions. It encompasses a wide range of digital financial services, including online banking, mobile payments, robo-advisors, peer-to-peer lending, and blockchain-based solutions. Fintech banks often operate without traditional physical branches, relying on digital platforms and automation to streamline processes, reduce costs, and improve the overall user experience. This disruption of traditional banking models has led to greater financial inclusion and convenience for consumers, as well as increased competition and innovation in the financial industry.

B) Definitions:

Following are the definitions of fintech banking

1) Chris Skinner:

"Fintech banking is the use of technology to deliver financial services in innovative and disruptive ways. It involves reimagining and redesigning traditional banking services by harnessing the power of digital tools, data analytics, and automation to create more efficient, customer-centric financial solutions."

2) Ben Robinson and Julian Skan:

"Fintech banking is the fusion of financial services with digital technology, aiming to create an improved customer experience, greater efficiency, and enhanced financial inclusion. It encompasses a broad spectrum of services, from mobile payments and peer-to-peer lending to AI-driven investment advice."

3) Brett King:

"Fintech banking is the democratization of finance through technology, where traditional financial institutions face competition from innovative startups that leverage data and digital platforms to deliver banking and financial services that are faster, cheaper, and more accessible to consumers."

C) Features of Fintech Banking:

Following are the features of fintech banking:

1) Digital-First Approach:

Fintech banking is characterized by a digital-first approach. It leverages online platforms, mobile apps, and web-based services to facilitate financial transactions and deliver banking services. This approach eliminates the need for physical branches, enabling users to manage their finances from the convenience of their devices.

2) User-Centric Design:

Fintech banks prioritize user experience and design. They create intuitive interfaces and user-friendly apps that make it easy for customers to navigate their financial accounts, conduct transactions, and access a range of financial services. The focus is on providing a seamless and enjoyable banking experience.

3) **Financial Inclusion:**
Fintech banking aims to increase financial inclusion by reaching underserved populations. Through digital channels, it offers financial services to individuals who may have limited access to traditional banking infrastructure, such as those in rural areas or with no prior banking history.

4) **Diverse Services:**
Fintech banks offer a wide range of services beyond traditional banking. These include online account opening, mobile payments, peer-to-peer lending, robo-advisors for investing, insurance technology (insurtech), and cryptocurrency services. The diversity of offerings caters to various financial needs.

5) **Personalization and AI:**
Fintech banks leverage artificial intelligence (AI) and machine learning to personalize services. They analyze customer data to provide tailored financial recommendations, investment strategies, and product suggestions. This personalization enhances customer engagement and satisfaction.

6) **Speed and Efficiency:**
Speed and efficiency are central to fintech banking. Digital processes streamline transactions, reducing the time it takes to complete financial tasks. This agility benefits users by providing quick access to funds and information.

7) **Security and Data Protection:**
Fintech banks prioritize security measures to protect user data and assets. They employ encryption, multi-factor authentication, and biometric recognition to ensure secure access to accounts. Compliance with data privacy regulations is also a key focus.

8) **Cost-Effective Solutions:**
Fintech banking often offers cost-effective alternatives to traditional banking. With lower overhead costs due to the absence of physical branches, fintech banks can offer competitive interest rates, reduced fees, and more favorable terms on loans and savings accounts.

9) **Global Reach and Cross-Border Transactions:**
Fintech banking facilitates cross-border transactions and international financial services. Users can send money abroad, make foreign currency exchanges, and access global investment opportunities with ease. This feature supports international trade and financial globalization.

10) **Disruptive Innovation:**
Fintech banking represents disruptive innovation in the financial industry. It challenges traditional banks to adapt and innovate in response to changing

customer expectations. This competition encourages financial institutions to improve their services and adopt digital technologies.

D) Challenges of Fintech Banking:

Here are key challenges of fintech banking:

1) Regulatory Compliance and Oversight:

Fintech banking operates in a highly regulated environment. Compliance with financial regulations, such as anti-money laundering (AML), know-your-customer (KYC) requirements, and data protection laws, is a formidable challenge. Fintech companies must navigate complex legal frameworks to ensure adherence to these rules, which can vary from one jurisdiction to another.

2) Cybersecurity Threats:

Fintech banks handle vast amounts of sensitive financial and personal data, making them prime targets for cyberattacks. Cybersecurity threats, including data breaches, ransomware attacks, and phishing attempts, pose significant risks to both customer trust and financial stability. Maintaining robust cybersecurity measures is paramount.

3) Data Privacy and Consumer Protection:

The collection and use of customer data by fintech banks raise concerns about data privacy and consumer protection. Striking a balance between providing personalized services through data analysis and safeguarding individuals' privacy rights is a challenge. Compliance with data protection regulations like GDPR or CCPA is crucial.

4) Scalability and Infrastructure:

As fintech banks grow and acquire more users, they must ensure their infrastructure can scale efficiently to accommodate increased transaction volumes and customer demands. Scaling up without service interruptions or performance degradation is a technical challenge.

5) Trust and Reputation Management:

Building and maintaining trust is vital in the financial sector. Fintech banks, often newcomers in the industry, must establish trust with customers who may be skeptical of digital-only banks. Ensuring reliability, transparency, and ethical practices is a continuous challenge.

6) Financial Inclusion and Accessibility:

While fintech banking has the potential to increase financial inclusion, it also faces the challenge of ensuring that its services are accessible to all, including those without access to the internet or digital literacy. Bridging this digital divide is essential for equitable access to financial services.

7) Competition and Market Saturation:

The fintech banking landscape is becoming increasingly competitive, with numerous players entering the market. As the market saturates, standing out and gaining market share becomes a challenge. Fintech companies must continually innovate to differentiate themselves.

8) **Interoperability and Integration:**

Fintech banks often need to integrate with legacy banking systems and other financial institutions. Achieving seamless interoperability between these diverse systems can be technically challenging. Compatibility and data exchange standards must be established.

9) **Funding and Capital Management:**

Many fintech startups face funding challenges, particularly in their early stages. Sourcing capital for expansion, innovation, and regulatory compliance can be difficult. Managing financial resources efficiently is crucial for long-term sustainability.

10) **Market and Regulatory Risks:**

Fintech banks are exposed to market risks, including fluctuations in interest rates and economic conditions. Additionally, regulatory changes can have a significant impact on their operations. Staying informed about and adapting to these risks is essential for long-term success.

2.5.5 Cloud Banking:

Cloud banking, also known as cloud-based banking, is a modern financial service model where banks utilize cloud computing technology to host and deliver their services. It enables banks to scale operations, enhance agility, and reduce infrastructure costs while providing customers with seamless access to banking services through web and mobile applications. Cloud banking offers the flexibility to adapt to changing customer demands and regulatory requirements, making it a key driver of innovation and efficiency in the banking industry.

A) **Meaning:**

Cloud banking, often referred to as cloud-based banking, is a financial service model where banks leverage cloud computing technology to store, manage, and deliver their services. By shifting their operations to the cloud, banks can streamline their processes, reduce infrastructure costs, and gain the flexibility to adapt quickly to changing market conditions. This approach allows customers to access banking services conveniently through web and mobile applications while ensuring data security and scalability. Cloud banking plays a pivotal role in modernizing the banking industry, enabling institutions to offer innovative and customer-centric solutions in an increasingly digital world.

B) **Definitions:**

Following are the definitions of the cloud banking:

1) **Deloitte:**
"Cloud banking refers to a banking model that relies on cloud computing technology for the delivery of various banking services. It involves using cloud infrastructure to host data, applications, and processes, allowing banks to achieve greater scalability, agility, and cost-efficiency."

2) **IBM:**
"Cloud banking is the practice of using cloud computing services and technologies to streamline and enhance various banking processes, including data storage, customer service, and application development. It enables banks to modernize their operations, reduce capital expenditures, and accelerate digital transformation."

3) **Finextra:**
"Cloud banking is a transformative approach to banking that leverages cloud technology to offer services and solutions over the internet. It involves migrating banking processes, data, and applications to cloud servers, enabling banks to provide scalable and innovative services while improving operational efficiency."

4) **McKinsey & Company:**
"Cloud banking represents a paradigm shift in the banking industry, where banks use cloud infrastructure to host their core banking systems and applications. This approach offers banks the ability to quickly adapt to market changes, reduce IT costs, and provide customers with modern, digitally-driven banking experiences."

C) **Features of Cloud Banking:**

Here are key features of cloud banking:

1) **Scalability:**
Cloud banking provides banks with the ability to scale their infrastructure and resources up or down based on demand. This flexibility is crucial in handling fluctuating workloads, accommodating growth, and efficiently managing peak transaction times, such as during holidays or special promotions.

2) **Cost Efficiency:**
One of the primary advantages of cloud banking is cost reduction. Banks can avoid significant upfront capital expenditures on physical infrastructure and hardware, as they can leverage the pay-as-you-go model offered by cloud providers. This cost efficiency extends to maintenance, as cloud providers handle system updates and maintenance tasks.

3) **Accessibility and Convenience:**
Cloud banking makes banking services accessible to customers 24/7 through web and mobile applications. Customers can perform transactions, check account balances, and access financial information from anywhere with an internet connection. This enhances convenience and improves the overall customer experience.

4) **Data Security and Compliance:**
Cloud banking providers prioritize data security and compliance with industry regulations. They invest in advanced security measures, encryption protocols, and access controls to protect customer data. Additionally, they often offer compliance features that help banks adhere to regulatory requirements.

5) **Rapid Deployment of Services:**
With cloud banking, banks can quickly launch new products and services without the lengthy hardware procurement and setup processes associated with traditional infrastructure. This agility enables banks to stay competitive in a rapidly evolving financial landscape.

6) **Disaster Recovery and Business Continuity:**
Cloud banking solutions include robust disaster recovery and business continuity plans. Data redundancy, backup systems, and failover mechanisms ensure that critical banking operations can continue even in the event of unforeseen disruptions or disasters.

7) **Advanced Analytics and Insights:**
Cloud banking platforms often integrate powerful analytics tools that allow banks to gain insights from customer data. These insights can inform product development, marketing strategies, risk assessment, and customer engagement efforts, leading to data-driven decision-making.

8) **Collaboration and Integration:**
Cloud banking facilitates collaboration with fintech partners and third-party providers. Banks can easily integrate innovative fintech solutions into their offerings, creating a diverse ecosystem of financial services. This fosters innovation and enables banks to offer customers a wider range of services.

9) **Customer-Centric Solutions:**
Cloud banking places a strong emphasis on creating customer-centric solutions. Banks can use data analytics and personalization techniques to tailor services to individual customer needs and preferences, enhancing customer satisfaction and loyalty.

10) **Regulatory Agility:**
Cloud banking solutions often include tools and features that help banks navigate complex regulatory landscapes. This agility is particularly important in the financial sector, where compliance with various regulations is crucial.

D) **Challenges Cloud Banking:**
Following are the challenges of cloud banking:

1) **Security and Compliance:**
Ensuring the security of financial data remains the foremost challenge for cloud banking. Banks are custodians of sensitive customer information and must comply

with strict regulatory standards. Cloud service providers (CSPs) must continually fortify their security measures to protect against data breaches, cyberattacks, and ensure adherence to industry-specific compliance requirements such as GDPR and PCI DSS.

2) **Data Privacy:**

Maintaining the privacy of customer data is a critical concern. Cloud banking platforms often involve the processing of vast amounts of personal and financial information. Banks must implement robust data encryption, access controls, and monitoring mechanisms to safeguard customer privacy. Additionally, they must navigate the complexities of data residency and international data transfer regulations.

3) **Cybersecurity Threats:**

The evolving landscape of cybersecurity threats poses an ongoing challenge for cloud banking. Malware, ransomware, and phishing attacks target both cloud infrastructure and customer data. Banks must invest in cutting-edge security technologies and continuously update their defense strategies to stay one step ahead of cybercriminals.

4) **Legacy Systems Integration:**

Many banks still rely on legacy systems that are incompatible with cloud technology. Integrating these systems with modern cloud-based solutions is a complex and costly process. Migration efforts require careful planning, and seamless integration is essential to maintain business continuity and minimize disruption to customers.

5) **Vendor Lock-In:**

Vendor lock-in is a risk associated with cloud banking, as institutions become heavily dependent on their chosen CSPs. Transitioning to a different provider can be challenging and expensive, making it imperative for banks to carefully evaluate vendor contracts and consider long-term implications.

6) **Scalability:**

Cloud banking offers scalability advantages, but managing rapid growth can be a double-edged sword. Banks must ensure that their cloud infrastructure can adapt to fluctuations in demand while maintaining service quality. Effective scalability requires a comprehensive strategy and robust monitoring tools.

7) **Cost Management:**

While cloud banking can reduce infrastructure costs, it also introduces new cost management challenges. Banks need to carefully track usage, optimize resource allocation, and avoid unnecessary expenses. Cloud cost management tools and strategies are vital to prevent budget overruns.

8) Regulatory Compliance:

The financial industry is heavily regulated, with rules that vary by region and are subject to change. Cloud banking institutions must continually monitor and adapt to evolving regulatory requirements. Ensuring compliance across all aspects of cloud operations, from data storage to disaster recovery, is a constant challenge.

9) Disaster Recovery and Business Continuity:

Maintaining robust disaster recovery and business continuity plans in a cloud environment is vital. Banks must be prepared for any unforeseen events, such as hardware failures, data breaches, or natural disasters, to ensure uninterrupted services and data integrity.

10) Talent Shortage:

The demand for skilled professionals who understand both cloud technology and the intricacies of the financial sector has surged. A shortage of such talent makes it difficult for banks to recruit and retain the experts needed to manage cloud banking solutions effectively.

2.5.6 Open Banking:

Open banking is a financial practice that allows third-party financial service providers to access and share customer financial data, with the customer's consent, through Application Programming Interfaces (APIs). It fosters competition, innovation, and the development of new financial services by enabling secure data sharing among banks and authorized fintech companies. Open banking empowers customers to have more control over their financial information and enables them to access a wider range of tailored financial products and services. This practice is driven by regulatory initiatives in many countries to promote transparency and enhance the banking experience for consumers.

A) Meaning:

Open banking is a financial practice that enables individuals and businesses to share their financial data securely with third-party financial service providers through standardized Application Programming Interfaces (APIs). This practice, often mandated or encouraged by regulatory authorities, promotes competition, innovation, and the development of new financial services by allowing authorized fintech companies and other institutions to access and utilize customer banking information, with the customer's explicit consent. It empowers consumers to have more control over their financial data, fosters the creation of personalized financial products, and enhances the overall banking experience by providing greater choice and convenience.

B) Definitions:

Following are the definitions of open banking:

1) **Deloitte:**

"Open banking is a system where banks and financial institutions provide access to their data to third-party providers through application programming interfaces (APIs). It allows for the sharing of financial information securely, enabling customers to grant permission to access their financial data to other financial institutions and fintech companies."

2) **World Bank:**

"Open banking is a financial services innovation that allows third-party financial service providers to access consumer financial data from banks through the use of APIs. This facilitates the development of new financial products and services and fosters competition in the financial industry."

3) **Capgemini:**

"Open banking is a banking practice that provides third-party financial service providers with access to consumer banking, transaction, and other financial data from banks and non-bank financial institutions through secure APIs. It enables the development of new services, fosters innovation, and improves customer experiences."

4) **McKinsey & Company:**

"Open banking is a banking ecosystem where banks collaborate with third-party providers to share customer data and payment services through APIs. This fosters competition, promotes innovation, and enhances customer choice and experience."

C) **Features of Open Banking:**

Following are the features of open banking:

1) **Data Sharing through APIs (Application Programming Interfaces):**

Open banking revolves around the secure sharing of customer financial data with third-party providers through APIs. APIs are the technological bridge that enables banks to expose their data to authorized entities while ensuring data security and privacy.

2) **Enhanced Customer Control:**

One of the fundamental principles of open banking is customer consent. It empowers customers to have greater control over their financial data. They can choose which third-party providers can access their data and for what purposes, creating a more personalized and secure banking experience.

3) **Increased Competition:**

Open banking encourages competition by allowing new players, such as fintech startups, to enter the financial services market. This competition can lead to better products, services, and pricing options for consumers, as traditional banks must innovate to stay competitive.

4) Innovation and Product Development:

With access to a broader range of financial data, third-party providers can develop innovative products and services. These may include budgeting apps, investment platforms, lending solutions, and more. Innovation flourishes as the industry becomes more collaborative and customer-centric.

5) Financial Inclusion:

Open banking has the potential to increase financial inclusion by making it easier for individuals and businesses to access financial services. Fintech companies can create solutions tailored to underserved or unbanked populations, expanding access to banking and credit.

6) Cross-Border Transactions:

Open banking has the capacity to simplify and expedite cross-border transactions. It can streamline international payments, reduce fees, and enhance the speed and transparency of global money transfers, benefiting businesses and consumers alike.

7) Regulatory Frameworks:

Regulatory bodies play a crucial role in shaping the open banking landscape. Many countries have implemented or are considering regulatory frameworks to govern data sharing, customer protection, and security standards. These frameworks help ensure a secure and standardized approach to open banking.

8) Security and Data Privacy:

Security is paramount in open banking. Banks and third-party providers must adhere to stringent security protocols to protect customer data from breaches and cyberattacks. Encryption, authentication, and authorization mechanisms are critical components of this security infrastructure.

9) Monetization Opportunities:

Open banking present's opportunities for financial institutions to monetize their data and APIs. Banks can charge third-party providers for access to their data, creating a new revenue stream. Additionally, they can explore partnerships with fintech companies to offer joint products and services.

10) Customer-Centric Banking:

Ultimately, open banking aims to shift the focus from the traditional product-centric approach to a customer-centric one. By allowing customers to share their data selectively, financial institutions can offer more personalized and tailored solutions that meet individual financial needs and preferences.

D) Challenges of Open Banking:

Following are the challenges of open banking:

1) Security and Data Privacy:

Open banking involves the sharing of sensitive financial data between banks and third-party providers. Ensuring the security and privacy of this data is paramount.

Cybersecurity threats, data breaches, and unauthorized access can have severe consequences for both customers and financial institutions. Developing robust security measures and compliance standards is an ongoing challenge.

2) **Regulatory Compliance:**
Open banking operates within a complex web of regulations and compliance requirements. Different regions and countries have their own regulatory frameworks, making it challenging for financial institutions to navigate and ensure they are in full compliance. Staying up-to-date with evolving regulations is an ongoing challenge, especially for multinational banks.

3) **Data Standardization:**
To enable seamless data sharing, there must be standardized data formats and structures. However, achieving consensus on data standards can be challenging, especially in a global context where different countries and regions may have varying requirements and preferences. Standardization is crucial to ensure interoperability and efficient data exchange.

4) **Consent Management:**
Central to open banking is customer consent for data sharing. Managing and tracking these consents across various third-party providers can be complex. Ensuring that customers have full control and visibility over their consents, and that these consents are honored and auditable, is a continuous challenge.

5) **API Development and Maintenance:**
The development and maintenance of robust and secure APIs are essential for open banking. Financial institutions need to invest in API infrastructure and ensure that these interfaces are reliable, scalable, and meet evolving technical standards. This requires ongoing investment and expertise in API management.

6) **Customer Education and Trust:**
Customers must understand the benefits and risks of open banking to make informed decisions. Building trust is crucial, and financial institutions and third-party providers need to invest in customer education and transparent communication about data sharing practices. Concerns about data privacy and security must be addressed to gain and maintain customer trust.

7) **Interoperability:**
Interoperability between various financial institutions, systems, and third-party providers is vital for the success of open banking. Ensuring that different platforms and technologies can seamlessly communicate and share data poses a significant technical challenge. Lack of interoperability can lead to fragmentation and hinder the development of innovative services.

8) **Liability and Dispute Resolution:**
Determining liability in cases of data breaches, fraud, or disputes between parties can be complex. Open banking involves multiple stakeholders, and clear guidelines

for liability and dispute resolution are essential. The absence of well-defined mechanisms can lead to legal disputes and regulatory challenges.

9) **Business Model Transformation:**

Traditional banks may need to transform their business models to adapt to the changing landscape of open banking. This transformation can be challenging, requiring investments in technology, talent, and a shift in organizational culture. Banks must also balance the desire for innovation with the need to protect existing revenue streams.

10) **Competitive Landscape:**

Open banking introduces new players into the financial ecosystem, including fintech startups and tech giants. This increased competition can pose challenges to traditional banks, as they may face pressure to offer competitive products and services while maintaining customer loyalty. Finding the right balance between collaboration and competition is a strategic challenge.

2.5.7 Neo Bank:

A neobank, also referred to as a digital bank or online bank, is a financial institution that operates exclusively or primarily through online and mobile platforms, devoid of physical branch locations. Neobanks leverage cutting-edge technology and user-friendly digital interfaces to provide a wide range of banking services, including savings accounts, checking accounts, payment processing, and loans. They prioritize convenience, accessibility, and often offer competitive fees or rates, aiming to disrupt traditional banking models and cater to the digital-savvy preferences of their customers. Neobanks have gained popularity for their agility, customer-centric approach, and commitment to redefining the banking experience in the digital age.

A) **Meaning:**

A neo bank, short for "new bank," refers to a digital or online-only financial institution that operates exclusively through digital platforms and mobile apps, often without traditional brick-and-mortar branches. Neo banks offer a range of banking services such as savings accounts, checking accounts, payment processing, and lending, aiming to provide customers with a convenient, tech-savvy, and customer-centric banking experience. Unlike traditional banks, neo banks typically have lower overhead costs, enabling them to offer competitive fees, better interest rates, and innovative financial products while prioritizing user-friendly digital interfaces and advanced financial technology solutions to enhance accessibility and efficiency in managing one's finances.

B) **Definitions:**

Following are the definitions of neo bank:

1) **Chris Skinner:**

"Neobanks are digital, branchless banks that offer banking services solely through online and mobile channels. They leverage technology to provide a seamless and customer-centric banking experience."

2) **Brett King:**

"Neobanks are the disruptors of traditional banking, characterized by their ability to deliver modern, user-friendly financial services through digital platforms, often with a focus on improved customer engagement and reduced fees."

3) **Ben Robinson:**

"Neobanks are a new breed of financial institutions that leverage technology, data, and customer-centric design to provide a range of banking and financial services to consumers and businesses. They are typically agile, tech-driven, and aim to challenge the status quo of traditional banking."

4) **The World Bank:**

"Neobanks are fintech-driven entities that provide banking services via digital channels, often without physical branches. They leverage technology to offer a range of financial products and services, catering to the evolving needs of a digitally-savvy customer base."

C) **Features of Neo Bank:**

Here are the key features of neo banks:

1) **Digital-First Approach:**

Neo banks are characterized by their digital-first approach. Unlike traditional banks with physical branches, neo banks operate entirely online or through mobile applications. Customers can access their accounts, make transactions, and manage their finances through their smartphones or computers.

2) **Seamless Account Opening:**

Opening an account with a neo bank is typically quick and easy. Customers can complete the entire onboarding process digitally, often in a matter of minutes. This convenience attracts users who are looking for a hassle-free banking experience.

3) **No Physical Branches:**

Neo banks do not have physical branch networks, which allows them to save on operating costs. This cost advantage is often passed on to customers in the form of lower fees and competitive interest rates on savings accounts and loans.

4) **Fee Transparency:**

Neo banks prioritize fee transparency, making it clear to customers what they will be charged for various services. Many neo banks offer fee-free accounts or have straightforward fee structures with no hidden charges. This transparency helps build trust with customers.

5) Personalized Financial Management:

Neo banks often provide advanced financial management tools to help customers better understand their spending habits and financial health. These tools may include budgeting features, expense categorization, and insights into saving and investing opportunities.

6) Innovative Payment Solutions:

Neo banks offer innovative payment solutions, such as virtual debit cards, digital wallets, and peer-to-peer (P2P) payment services. These features make it easier for customers to send money, pay bills, and make online purchases.

7) Global Accessibility:

Many neo banks offer international banking services, allowing customers to send and receive money across borders with lower fees compared to traditional banks. Some neo banks even provide multi-currency accounts and international payment options.

8) Customer-Centric Approach:

Neo banks prioritize the customer experience by offering 24/7 customer support through digital channels. They often rely on data-driven insights to tailor their services to individual customer needs, leading to a more personalized banking experience.

9) Partnerships and Integrations:

Neo banks frequently collaborate with fintech companies and other service providers to offer a wide range of financial products and services. These partnerships may include insurance, investment opportunities, and access to third-party apps that enhance the overall banking experience.

10) Regulatory Compliance:

While neo banks operate primarily in the digital space, they still adhere to financial regulations and security standards to ensure the safety of customer funds and data. Neo banks typically use encryption and authentication methods to protect customer information.

D) Challenges of Neo Bank:

Here are the key challenges faced by neo banks:

1) Regulatory Compliance and Licensing:

Neo banks must navigate complex and evolving regulatory landscapes in various jurisdictions. Obtaining the necessary licenses and complying with regulatory requirements can be time-consuming and costly. Additionally, regulatory changes can impact their business models and require ongoing adaptations.

2) **Customer Acquisition and Retention**:
Gaining and retaining customers can be challenging in a highly competitive market. Neo banks often rely on digital marketing and word-of-mouth to attract users. Building trust and loyalty in a digital-only environment is essential, and the lack of physical branches can be a barrier for some customers.

3) **Monetization and Revenue Generation**:
Many neo banks offer fee-free or low-fee accounts to attract customers, making it challenging to generate sufficient revenue to cover operating costs and achieve profitability. Finding sustainable monetization strategies, such as offering premium services or cross-selling financial products, is a constant challenge.

4) **Security and Fraud Prevention**:
As digital entities, neo banks are susceptible to cybersecurity threats and fraud. Ensuring robust security measures and fraud prevention systems is critical to protect customer funds and data. A single security breach can severely damage their reputation.

5) **Scale and Infrastructure**:
Scaling operations while maintaining service quality is a significant challenge for neo banks. As their customer base grows, they need to invest in infrastructure, including servers, technology, and customer support, to handle increased demand effectively.

6) **Credit Risk and Lending**:
Neo banks that offer lending services face challenges in assessing and managing credit risk. Without traditional credit history data, they must rely on alternative data sources and advanced algorithms to make lending decisions. Striking a balance between responsible lending and profitability is crucial.

7) **Dependence on Third-Party Providers**:
Neo banks often rely on third-party providers for various services, such as payment processing, customer support, and regulatory compliance tools. Over-dependence on these partners can lead to operational vulnerabilities and potential disruptions if a partner encounters issues.

8) **Market Saturation and Competition**:
The neo banking space has become increasingly crowded, with numerous players vying for market share. Competition is intense, and new entrants face the challenge of differentiating themselves and offering unique value propositions to stand out.

9) **Global Expansion and Localization**:
Expanding operations across borders requires dealing with different regulatory environments, languages, and cultural nuances. Adapting products and services to cater to local preferences while maintaining a consistent brand identity can be a complex endeavor.

10) Long-Term Profitability:

Achieving sustainable profitability is perhaps the most significant challenge for neo banks. Many startups in this space operate at a loss initially as they invest in growth and customer acquisition. The path to profitability can be uncertain, and investors may have high expectations.

♦♦♦

Multiple Choice Questions

1) **Digital banking allows customers to perform transactions through ------------ channels.**
   a) Traditional b) Physical c) Manual d) Online
2) **Mobile banking apps provide users with the convenience of banking on their ------------ devices.**
   a) Virtual b) Physical c) Automated d) Mobile
3) **Digital banks often rely on advanced ------------ for secure and efficient transactions.**
   a) Technology b) Documents c) Procedures d) Processes
4) **Biometric authentication, such as fingerprint and facial recognition, enhances digital banking ------------.**
   a) Innovation b) Transactions c) Security d) Accessibility
5) **Digital banking transforms the customer experience by offering real-time ------------ and personalized services.**
   a) Data b) Documents c) Transactions d) Traditional
6) **Cybersecurity aims to protect digital banking systems from unauthorized access, data breaches, and ------------.**
   a) Innovation b) Compliance c) Threats d) Efficiency
7) **Phishing attacks involve deceptive techniques to trick users into disclosing sensitive ------------.**
   a) Innovations b) Compliance c) Information d) Transactions
8) **Malware, such as viruses and trojans, poses a significant ------------ to the integrity of digital banking systems.**
   a) Compliance b) Innovation c) Threat d) Efficiency
9) **Social engineering exploits human psychology to manipulate users into divulging confidential ------------.**
   a) Innovations b) Compliance c) Information d) Transactions

10) Two-factor authentication enhances digital banking security by adding an extra layer of ------------.

a) Threat b) Innovation c) Compliance d) Authentication

11) The dark web is a potential source for cybercriminals to buy and sell stolen ------------.

a) Threats b) Innovations c) Compliance d) Transactions

12) DoS attacks aim to disrupt digital banking services by overwhelming them with excessive ------------.

a) Innovations b) Transactions c) Compliance d) Traffic

13) The National Cyber Security Policy (NCSP) outlines a country's strategic approach to addressing cyber ------------.

a) Threats b) Innovations c) Compliance d) Transactions

14) Insider threats involve malicious actions by individuals within the organization who exploit their ------------.

a) Innovations b) Transactions c) Compliance d) Access

15) Regular cybersecurity training for employees is crucial to create awareness and mitigate the risk of human-related ------------.

a) Innovations b) Threats c) Transactions d) Compliance

16) Blockchain technology ensures secure and transparent transactions through decentralized and distributed ------------.

a) Networks b) Data c) Platforms d) Innovations

17) Artificial Intelligence (AI) in banking improves customer service through predictive analytics and personalized ------------.

a) Compliance b) Innovations

c) Recommendations d) Transactions

18) Banking industry adoption of robots streamlines routine tasks and enhances operational ------------.

a) Compliance b) Innovations c) Efficiency d) Transactions

19) Digital Rupee represents India's exploration of a central bank digital currency (CBDC) to digitize and modernize the ------------.

a) Transactions b) Innovations c) Currency d) Compliance

20) Fintech banking integrates technology to offer innovative financial products and services, challenging ------------ banking.

a) Traditional b) Compliance c) Innovations d) Neo

21) Cloud banking leverages cloud infrastructure to provide scalable, flexible, and cost-effective financial ------------.

a) Innovations b) Platforms c) Transactions d) Compliance

22) Open banking promotes collaboration between financial institutions and third-party providers, fostering greater ------------ and competition.

a) Innovations b) Compliance c) Efficiency d) Transactions

23) Neo banks, as digital-only entities, offer banking services without ------------ branches.

a) Compliance b) Innovations c) Physical d) Transactions

24) Blockchain's smart contracts automate and enforce contractual agreements, reducing the need for ------------ intermediaries.

a) Compliance b) Innovations c) Traditional d) Physical

25) AI-powered chatbots in banking provide instant customer support, improving user experience and reducing response ------------.

a) Time b) Innovations c) Compliance d) Transactions

26) Robo-advisors use algorithms to provide personalized investment advice, disrupting traditional ------------ management.

a) Compliance b) Innovations c) Wealth d) Transactions

27) Digital Rupee aims to enhance financial ------------ and reduce dependence on physical currency.

a) Innovations b) Compliance c) Inclusion d) Transactions

28) Fintech banking platforms offer innovative solutions such as peer-to-peer lending and contactless ------------ options.

a) Innovations b) Transactions c) Compliance d) Payment

29) Cloud banking ensures data security and accessibility, enabling financial institutions to scale their operations with ------------.

a) Innovations b) Compliance c) Efficiency d) Transactions

30) Open banking initiatives allow customers to share their financial data securely with third-party providers for more personalized ------------.

a) Innovations b) Transactions

c) Recommendations d) Compliance

Ans : **1)** d, **2)** d, **3)** a, **4)** c, **5)** a, **6)** c, **7)** c, **8)** c, **9)** c, **10)** d, **11)** c, **12)** d, **13)** a, **14)** d, **15)** b, **16)** a, **17)** c, **18)** c, **19)** c, **20)** a, **21)** b, **22)** a, **23)** c, **24)** c, **25)** a, **26)** c, **27)** c, **28)** d, **29)** a, **30)** c.

◆◆◆

Review Questions

Q.1. Answer the Following Questions:

1) What is mean by Digital Banking? Explain the features of Digital Banking.
2) Discuss about the benefits of Digital Banking.
3) Explain the Technological Development in Banking Delivery Channels.
4) Discuss about the Technological Development in Payment Systems.
5) What is mean by Cyber Security? Explain need of Cyber Security.
6) Explain the challenges of Cyber Security.
7) Discuss about the National Cyber Security Policy (NCSP).
8) What is mean by Block Chain? Explain features of Block Chain.
9) Discuss about the challenges of Block Chain.
10) What is mean by Artificial Intelligence Robots? Explain features of Artificial Intelligence Robots.
11) Explain the challenges of Artificial Intelligence Robots.
12) What is mean by Digital Rupee? Explain features of Digital Rupee.
13) Explain the challenges of Digital Rupee.
14) What is mean by Fintech Banking? Explain features of Fintech Banking.
15) Discuss in detail about the challenges of Fintech Banking.
16) What is mean by Cloud Banking? Explain features of Cloud Banking.
17) Explain in detail challenges of Cloud Banking.
18) What is mean by Open Banking? Explain features of Open Banking.
19) Discuss the challenges of Open Banking.
20) What is mean by Neo Bank? Explain the features of Neo Bank.
21) Explain the challenges of Neo Bank.

Q.2. Write Short Notes on:

1) Digital Banking.
2) Cyber Security.
3) National Cyber Security Policy.
4) Block Chain.
5) Artificial Intelligence Robots.
6) Digital Rupee.
7) Fintech Banking.
8) Cloud Banking.
9) Open Banking.
10) Neo Banking.

♦♦♦

NOTES